# STOP
## SUCKING
## AT **SALES**

# STOP SUCKING AT **SALES**

## 15 SECRETS
### TO MAKE YOU A BETTER SALESPERSON TODAY

**BRIAN NEWMAN**
with STEPHEN NEWMAN

Copyright © 2015 by Brian Newman
ALL RIGHTS RESERVED

*Managing Editor*
Kris Reisdorf

*Design and Production*
Erin Akiko Shishido

ISBN 978-1-5033-6036-5

Printed in the US

*To my dad,
for encouraging me to do whatever I
wanted, and welcoming me with open
arms when I decided I wanted to do
what he did.*

# Contents

| | |
|---|---|
| i | Foreword |
| 1 | Introduction<br>SALES 101—NOBODY GOES TO SCHOOL TO BECOME A SALESPERSON |
| 5 | Secret #1<br>DON'T HIDE BEHIND EMAIL |
| 20 | Secret #2<br>"FREE TRIALS" ARE FOR LOSERS |
| 27 | Secret #3<br>OVERPREPARE FOR EVERY MEETING<br>(PRIOR PREPARATION PREVENTS PISS-POOR PERFORMANCE) |
| 46 | Secret #4<br>SHUT UP AND LISTEN |
| 55 | Secret #5<br>MASTER BODY LANGUAGE |
| 66 | Secret #6<br>DON'T JUST SELL ONE BANANA<br>(SELL THE WHOLE PLANTATION!) |
| 76 | Secret #7<br>YOU ARE NOT A VENDOR |
| 87 | Secret #8<br>FUTURE. POSITIVE. |
| 98 | Secret #9<br>ROLE-PLAY |
| 103 | Secret #10<br>STOP TRYING TO MULTITASK—YOU SUCK AT IT |
| 108 | Secret #11<br>SELL IDEAS |
| 126 | Secret #12<br>CELEBRATE WINS, FORGET DEFEATS |
| 140 | Secret #13<br>KEEP A DIARY |
| 144 | Secret #14<br>THE PERFECT WEEK |
| 155 | Secret #15<br>TRAIN THE BODY WITH THE MIND |
| 162 | The Final Secret |
| 168 | In Closing |

# Foreword

I never told my son that he should be a salesman, never even suggested it. He went to college and studied Asian languages and literature, and then moved to Asia for good at the age of 25. Then one day he called me and said, "Dad, I just got a job in sales." I couldn't have been more surprised; I figured he was going to end up a professor someday.

I've trained hundreds of salespeople during my 30-year career as a salesman, sales manager, and CEO. And I've distilled all those many years of teaching and training down to a few fundamental "secrets" that are universal. They apply no matter who you are, where you are, or what you are selling.

My son started calling me to ask questions about challenges he faced in his day-to-day sales career in Tokyo, and we had long conversations where I described to him the secrets that had made me a successful salesperson and defined every successful salesperson I knew.

"This stuff is golden," he told me one day. "You should write it down in a book."

"Tell you what," I said, "You make these secrets work for you and we'll write it together."

And he did.

And we did.

The secrets aren't complicated. They are very simple actually. They worked for my dad before me, and they worked for me and my son, and they will work for you. The economy fluctuates, technology marches on, but the rules of engagement have not changed.

Keep reading—I'm going to tell you 15 secrets that will make you, like my son, a world-class salesperson.

Stephen Newman
Knoxville, TN
April 2014

# Introduction

## SALES 101—NOBODY GOES TO SCHOOL TO BECOME A SALESPERSON

Why doesn't anyone go to college to become a salesperson? Ask a bunch of 10-year-olds what they want to be when they grow up: doctors, pilots, presidents of the free world. We've never heard a little kid say that when he grows up he wants to work five days a week selling anything. Not selling used cars, not selling arms to Middle Eastern dictatorships, definitely not selling a product that somebody else invented to somebody who has never heard of it.

Sales sounds cheap. Selling things to people who don't really need the things you're selling. But if you're smooth, clever, slimy enough, you might be able to make a sale to a few unsuspecting fools. Or a lot of unsuspecting fools—ratio of ability to sell directly proportionate to your level of depravity as a human being.

There are not, as far as we know, any classes in "selling" taught at the world's top universities. Selling 101, now that is probably a course you are not going to take. Course topics: the cold call, proposal writing, the false time constraint close ("If you don't come see me *today*, I can't save you any money!"[*]). But how about Selling Yourself 101? We might take that one. Course topics: being irresistible to others in bars, getting extra shots of espresso from a barista, smiling your way to business class upgrades.

Barring low-ticket, mass-produced, one-off transactional sales (think McDonald's; total time of sale: 30 seconds, moments of actual eye contact: zero), the act of selling a complex product, solution, or service includes a large element of human interaction. We humans don't usually buy stuff from people who we despise, and the inverse of that is also true. We are more likely to buy from people we like.

Successful sales engagements, which we can define as happy sellers *and* happy buyers, are always relationship sales. In other words, these sales always include an element of meaningful human interaction.

You've heard that old adage that prostitution is the world's oldest profession? Wrong. Sales is the world's oldest profession. Every act involves someone asking "How much?" and someone saying a price. Sales.

This is where we think salespeople face a social stigma, and why most of the kids in the elementary school playground have notions of entering the more "honorable" professions like politicians or rappers. There is a sense that one is born into sales, that it is an art or a genetic trait. Sales DNA cannot be taught, so there's

---

[*] "If you don't come see me today, I can't save you any money!" was the annoying yet effective kicker in early 90s television commercials of Scott Thomason, owner of Thomason Auto Group in Portland, Oregon. My friends and I, the whole town in fact, went around quoting his famous "time constraint close" whenever we had the chance.

no need to formally train through pre-career schooling, right?

Wrong.

For a profession that has no formal undergraduate curriculum available, there are a huge number of global practitioners. Every single company in the world that provides a product, platform, solution, or service will have a significant portion of its workforce in sales. Show us a company without a sales force, and we'll show you a chief executive officer, president, or head of marketing who does a hell of a lot of selling.

And because about 90 percent of those salespeople don't have a clue what they are doing—they are out there trying to get business class upgrades with a winning smile and well-tailored suit—a whole cottage industry in on-the-job sales training has arisen.

We've taken a lot of these courses, delivered by some of the best sales organizations and training programs in the world. The fact is that these courses are delivered on the job and primarily focused on how to sell that company's products or services. When really what we need are fundamental grounding principles of sales that can be applied to any industry or product, what we get are some very specific techniques for selling some very specific products or services.

**PRINCIPLE**: gravity
**TECHNIQUE**: building a spaceship

As father and son, we have a combined 55 years of sales experience between the two of us, with on-the-ground, in-the-trenches sales and sales team management in the US, UK, Japan, China, Hong Kong, Korea, Singapore, and Australia. We're going to start with the principles that are universal for any type of sales, and we're going to give you real life examples of each of these principles in practice. We're going to build techniques off those principles, and describe pitfalls and how to avoid them.

We are product, service, solution, platform agnostic. We don't have any favorite horses; we pick them all to win. We have sold everything from beer, to timeshare rentals, to TV advertising, to complex IT systems, to companies. This book will be useful no matter what you sell. You can read it front to back, or for the more experienced of you, cherry-pick certain sections in which you're interested.

Sales is a romantic profession. Fine wines, expensive suits, deals done in back rooms. Sales professionals are perceived as artists, structuring complex deals out of thin air, waving a hand to make an order appear.

The reality is that behind the romance, behind the "art" of sales, there is a science, and the most successful salespeople have mastered this. We're going to teach you that science.

You'll be 50 percent better at selling after reading this book or 110 percent of your money back. If you don't read this today, we can't make you any money...

# Secret #1

## DON'T HIDE BEHIND EMAIL

*Email has its uses, but it should never be used in lieu of a meaningful human interaction with your prospects, your clients, or for that matter, your boyfriend or girlfriend. Stop sending emails, nobody is reading them anyway!*

We said in the intro that we have 55 years of sales experience behind us. Guess what office technology was used for at least half of Dad's career in sales?

Desk phone. Copy machine.

That's it. All those big Fortune 500 companies that Warren Buffett buys for billions of dollars? They started with four things. Great people. Great ideas. Desk phone. Copy machine.

Now the automobile has been around a lot longer than the phone, and a lot of those great people had cars. So the way they sold was they got in the car and they drove over to visit prospective clients. Sometimes they called first, but most of the time they didn't. They learned quickly that it was easy for that prospect to say no over the phone, but a lot harder when you were sitting there chatting to their secretary, hat in hand, politely asking for 10 minutes of their time.

We've talked about successful sales engagements (happy buyers *and* happy sellers) always having an element of meaningful human interaction. Let's look at levels of human interaction through the following mediums.

Forget about sales for a minute. Imagine you are asking someone to marry you.

**TEXT:** hey babe, been thinking, tie the knot with me? luv u —J

**EMAIL:** Hi Cindy, I've been doing a lot of thinking, and I just feel so complete when we're together. I want to spend the rest of my life with you. Will you marry me?

**PHONE:** "Hey, hon, it's so great to hear your voice (sighs), I've been missing you so much (laughs nervously). Hon, there's something I've been wanting to ask you, and I think now is the time (long pause). I-I-I want to spend the rest of my life with you (breathless), I love you and I want you to marry me.

**FACE-TO-FACE:** (Looking deep into Cindy's eyes) "Baby, I love you and want to spend the rest of my life with you. Please marry me and make me the happiest man alive." (Hug. Cindy feels the pounding of his heart and starts to cry tears of joy.)

We do not know anyone who proposed to their spouse over text, email, or Facebook, and seriously hope you do not either.

## Secret #1: DON'T HIDE BEHIND EMAIL

Most important things that you do in your life should be done face-to-face. Is sales important to you?

Well, you're reading this book.

When you got your current job did you get it over email? Nope, you got it by having several interviews with key stakeholders in the company who made a gut-wrenching decision based on a 60-minute interview about what kind of person you are.

Would you quit a job by sending an email to your boss? How would you feel if you were the boss and got that email? How would you feel if you were Cindy and got a breakup text? Hiding behind email is not just bad manners, it is a crutch of bad salespeople who are not willing or able to master essential skills in human interaction.

Email does have its uses. It allows you to deliver pricing or proposals quickly with a written record for future reference. It's an easy way to fine-tune schedules once a meeting has already been confirmed by phone or face-to-face. In other words, it is a workflow tool that can bring some efficiency to the sales process and free up more of your time for meaningful human interactions.

> ### "STOP SENDING US EMAILS!"
> I conducted a training session for a dozen business owners recently who wanted to know how to effectively buy advertising for their businesses. I asked them some questions about their understanding of the changes that were taking place in media (radio, TV, digital, online, direct mail, out-of-door, place-based media) and the answers were consistent with what the average person

> would understand based on their use of that media. Then I asked, "Who do you depend on to keep you up to speed on changes that are happening in your market when it comes to media?"
>
> The answers were astonishing: Their spouses, friends, networking groups, and, lastly, their media rep. Many said that they did not enjoy meeting their media reps because the reps just wanted to know if they were going to get a buy in any particular month. They said they saw their reps every few months at the most.
>
> "If you don't see them except every couple months, how do they communicate with you?" I asked.
>
> Answer: email.
>
> "How do you like that?" I went on.
>
> Answer: "Hate it."
>
> They told me that they hate email and rarely read more than the first few words, only about as much as they can see on the screens of their phone without scrolling down.
>
> "How would you prefer they communicate with you?" I asked my final question.
>
> "Tell them to call us," the business owners said. "Tell them to come see us, walk into our place of business, sit down for a chat, get to know us so that you can advise us better. Stop sending us emails. We're not reading them anyway."

## USING EMAIL EFFECTIVELY AS A WORKFLOW TOOL

*The 4-Hour Work Week* by Tim Ferriss is a great read on how to use email effectively. Ferriss gets pretty extreme

Secret #1: **DON'T HIDE BEHIND EMAIL**

in advocating checking email for only one hour per week, which is probably not practical for most of us. We always get a little chuckle imagining the following office exchange:

## FERRISS' RULES

1. Wean yourself down to checking emails two or three times a day for 30 minutes or an hour at most each time. All other times keep your email off. If you are worried about missing urgent emails, set up an auto reply that directs people to your phone if they need to reach you urgently.

2. Never use email for something that could be easily decided over a brief phone call or face-to-face meeting.

3. Never use email for something that is going to be a difficult decision to make and require serious thought and discussion.

That's it. Do it for a week. A day isn't enough to get over the addiction to the gotta-check-my-email itch.

You'll quickly find that all those "urgent" emails you were getting weren't urgent at all. What you were really doing was using email like a live chat, going back and forth over several emails about something that could have been solved by one thoughtful, well-written email, or better yet, a three-minute phone call, or a two-minute face-to-face meeting.

Now, since you have just freed up six or seven hours of your workday from mindless email, start your day with a top priority and middle priority to-do list. A few items on each, the top priorities are the ones that you absolutely must get done today, and will be largely weighted towards human interactions: client meetings and client phone calls.

You know what this leaves you with now? Desk phone. Copy machine. And a list of people you want to meet and call today.

*Hiding behind email is not just bad manners, it is a crutch of bad salespeople who are not willing or able to master essential skills in human interaction.*

After a week of this, you'll find that you're getting through your top priorities by noon, and that you will dramatically increase your number of human interactions. You have also freed up time to be thoughtful, strategic, and extremely overprepared for important meetings (more on this later).

Secret #1: DON'T HIDE BEHIND EMAIL

## USING EMAIL TO MAKE A COLD CALL WARM

Cold calling a prospect is one of the most challenging things you will do as a salesperson. Email can be an elegant way to make a cold call slightly warm. The email should deliver a very simple intro and relevant statement, concluding with a commitment to call later for follow-up. Keep it short. Most of your prospects are reading this on their phones because they are out of the office having meaningful human interactions.

**COLD EMAIL EXAMPLE**

> Ross,
>
> I look after the client coverage team for (name of your company). We're doing some innovative work around targeting private companies ripe for equity capital raising, and I was hoping I could have 15 minutes of your time to run this by you. I'll call later today to see if we can schedule something.
>
> Regards,
> Brian

- **THREE SENTENCES**
  Who I am, what I do that Ross might be interested in, what I'm asking for. Even Ross, who runs the IPO (initial public offering) team at a major global investment bank and is always on the road pitching to new prospects has the time to read this entire email on his phone and doesn't have to scroll down

to do it.

> *Keep it short. Most of your prospects are reading this on their phones because they are out of the office having meaningful human interactions.*

- **DON'T TRY TO BEAT THE STIGMA OF "SALES"**
  Work around it. Salespeople cover clients, you cover clients, you are therefore a coverage person, which sounds a lot less threatening than a salesperson.

- **YOU HAVE RESEARCHED ROSS WELL**
  You know that he runs the IPO team at a major global investment bank and is a salesperson like you, always looking for qualified prospects (in this case, private companies that are looking to go public), so you are offering to tell him about something that could be tremendously valuable to his business.

- **NOTHING ABOUT THIS EMAIL SAYS "SALES"**
  You are demonstrating in just a few words that you know what Ross does and that you have something you think would be useful for him, which you want to "run by him." You are not saying you want to present to him; you are not saying you want to introduce your product to him. Both those statements sound like long boring PowerPoint presentations that we don't want to hear. Other substitutions for "run by you" are "sanity check with you" and "get your feedback on." Both of those variations appeal to Ross' position as an expert in the field, and someone

whose opinion you value.

- **YOU HAVE OFFERED UP A REASSURING (PROBABLY FALSE) TIME CONSTRAINT**
  We are not suggesting that you are being disingenuous here with the 15 minutes statement. You will walk into that meeting fully prepared to get through the agenda in 15 minutes. That said, since your agenda is going to be a lot of asking Ross about Ross, and because Ross might like to talk about himself, the meeting is going to take a lot longer than 15 minutes. Other than world leaders and celebrities, who sets a 15-minute meeting anyway? No matter how you schedule that into a calendar, it looks like a 30-minute slot. We often use "10 minutes" or "just a few minutes" for hard-to-reach prospects to reassure them that they can get out of the meeting quickly if they want.

If you have researched Ross and you don't think you have something he might be interested in, don't email or call him until you do.

A few hours after sending this email you are going to call Ross and say, "Ross, this is Brian from (company name). I sent you an email earlier today." Ross will remember you, you will get the meeting. Be prepared to go into more detail on the offering you described in email, as he may want to qualify whether you are worth 15 minutes of his time.

With a strong succinct email like this, you'll often get the meeting without a phone call. Make the phone call.

Just like you warmed Ross up for the call with an email, you're warming him up for the future meeting with a call.

Secret #1: **DON'T HIDE BEHIND EMAIL**

### Dad's Story
### HOUSTON, WE HAVE A PROBLEM

Never mistake an email to a potential client for real contact. There are simply too many executives who do not read their emails.

I had a young salesperson, we will call him Houston, who so believed in the power of email that he spent several hours every workday sending all kinds of emails. On one occasion he told me that he had received a great deal of interest in our product from a government agency. We talked about the prospect and it came out that they were located about 200 miles from our office. I asked him to call the agency to set up a meeting, and we would drive out together.

A week later I asked about the meeting and he said that they hadn't responded to any of his emails. "Okay, what did they say when you called them?" I asked.

"I didn't call them," Houston told me. "We've been talking over email."

I asked him to get the phone number and bring it to my office.

I called the secretary who Houston had been corresponding with, Sara, and got the name of the director she worked for, and told her that I was going to be in their city the following Tuesday and asked for a 15-minute meeting.

"Sure, we look forward to seeing you," she told me, and we were off and running.

Houston and I drove the 200 miles and turned that 15-minute meeting slot into a one-hour meeting with the director. Funding was not in yet, but they were very interested in our product, and just needed a better indication of how much funding they would get and then they could commit.

All good.

Fast-forward four months.

"Houston, where are we with the DOT buy?"

"I haven't heard back yet on whether their funding came through."

"When was the last time you talked to them?"

Long silence. Crickets chirping.

"Houston, when was the last time you spoke to Sara?"

He looked at me sheepishly. "We've been emailing at least once a month."

The director of the agency had called an all-comers media day and had asked for proposals from all of his reps. Houston had not been well-connected with the prospect through the emails he kept sending them, and we hadn't been invited to the meeting.

Houston was crushed that he had lost the business, but sometimes the hardest lessons are the best ones, and he became my top guy on the phone. He read every book he could find on cold calling and persuasion and elevator pitches, and dedicated himself to becoming good on the phone and asked me to role-play with him over and over again. He became one of my best sales guys and I promoted him to manage his own sales team.

Some years after his loss, when he was a successful salesperson and excellent sales team manager in his own right, he came into my office and said, "Steve, you've got to help me out with Jimmy. This guy spends all day on email. I asked him when he had last spoken to the Knowles account and he said he sent them an email but hadn't heard back yet..."

# Secret #1: DON'T HIDE BEHIND EMAIL

### Son's Story
### THE POWERFUL PERSONAL ASSISTANT

Try getting a meeting with someone who works at Goldman Sachs. It isn't easy. Now try getting a meeting with someone who works at Goldman Sachs, and try getting it totally cold. You don't know the guy, don't know his phone number or email. You don't know anyone who knows him who could make an introduction. To say this isn't easy would be a vast understatement. When it comes to getting a meeting, this is about as hard as it gets.

This was my dilemma. I needed to get in front of Mark, one of the most senior Goldman Sachs executives in Hong Kong. My company had spent millions on R & D (research and development) to come up with a game-changing product for his business. We were fairly confident that—if we could just get a meeting—this great new product would virtually sell itself.

What were my options here?

I could guess at Mark's email address until I got it right and send him a cold email suggesting a meeting. Keep in mind that he is one of the most powerful captains of banking in Hong Kong. How many emails do you get a day? A lot? Well I promise you that Mark gets more. Nothing that I wrote or sent was going to shine through the mass of emails to get his attention. In my experience, the odds of getting a reply to an email like that are one in a hundred. Not good odds.

I could try to tap my network to find someone who knew Mark and could make an introduction. This is a viable approach. But young sales professionals and 55-year-old Goldman Sachs masters of the universe traverse in very different social and professional circles, and I drew a blank trying to find an "in" this way.

I could try to work my way up to Mark by first meeting junior people on his team. This process involves meeting a junior banker and impressing him with the amazing product so that he agrees to put you up a notch to his manager. This could potentially get me to Mark after three or four meetings, but I didn't like this approach for two reasons.

One, it was going to take more time than I was willing to spend. At least several months, probably many more as most of these guys are road warriors who live in Cathay Pacific business class.

The second reason that I didn't like this approach was that each of those meetings with Mark's juniors in Goldman Sachs was a potential chance for failure. If someone along the way didn't like what I was selling, it would become that much more difficult to ultimately get to Mark. "I don't think this is something that we'd be interested in" spelled a death knell for my sales strategy.

I could cold call Mark on the telephone. I was fairly confident that if I could get him on the phone, my two-minute elevator pitch was going to pique his interest enough that he would agree to meet me.

Have you ever tried calling the general line for Goldman Sachs and asking the receptionist to put you through to one of their most senior bankers? It doesn't work.

What I did know was Mark's department though, so the plan I came up with was to get to Mark's personal assistant (I wasn't sure that he had one, but in my experience, executives in his position always do) and get the meeting through her. I called the department and asked for Mark's personal assistant. Sandra came on the line, and while she was a gatekeeper who had to filter out the relevant from

## Secret #1: DON'T HIDE BEHIND EMAIL

the unworthy, she wasn't in a position to filter me because she herself wasn't able to judge whether my pitch had merit or not.

I told her briefly what I wanted to speak to Mark about, and asked for 15 minutes in his calendar, and she asked me to send her an email with that in writing and she would check with him. She was very professional; I was very polite. I emailed her and called her back two days later to check in, and although she hadn't spoken to Mark yet, she did find me 15 minutes in his calendar the following week. I was careful to come across as credible and knowledgeable about their business and department, and Sandra decided that I probably merited a few minutes of Mark's time.

The meeting with Mark went well and we had several meetings after that. I always followed the same pattern of getting the meetings through Sandra and she ultimately introduced me to other executive assistants within Goldman Sachs to help me meet more partners. I'm sure it didn't hurt that, as is customary in Asian cultures, most times I visited, I brought a box of chocolates or some other small gift to thank her for all her help with coordination.

Never underestimate the power of the personal assistant.

# Secret #2

## "FREE TRIALS" ARE FOR LOSERS

*If you want to give something away, forget the "trial" part and just give it away. Free trials are a last resort for unskilled salespeople who can't articulate what they are selling.*

Unable to "sell" the product/service/platform, the salesperson gives his product away hoping that it will speak for itself better than he can. So why do you need the salesperson at all? An inexpensive office administrator could schedule a free trial over email and write up a quote and take an order. And the boss doesn't even have to pay the office administrator a commission.

Win win!

No, lose lose.

Lose because you have now become a purveyor of goods without any human interaction. Your product, which was offered without a value attached, is now worth exactly the value you, the salesperson, attached to it. In other words, it's worthless. When it comes time to move from free trial to paid product, the client is going to be unwilling to pay for something that they were getting for free. It has now become much harder to sell than it was before the client was given the free trial.

## Secret #2: "FREE TRIALS" ARE FOR LOSERS

There are only two reasons why a client will request a free trial:

1. **SHE WANTS TO ASSESS PRODUCT USABILITY**
   - Is it easy or intuitive to use?
   - Does it work the way I want it to work?

2. **SHE WANTS TO ASSESS PRODUCT QUALITY**
   - Does it work as advertised?
   - Is the quality worth the price?

These two objections and "try before I buy" requests can be deflected in two simple ways:

1. **SCHEDULE A DEMO OR VALIDATION SESSION**
   Your product expert skillfully walks the prospect through actual usage and answers questions. This might mean visiting the prospect's office and sitting in a room for half of a day while different stakeholders come in and out to assess usability and play around with the product themselves.

2. **OFFER SAMPLES**
   Instead of letting prospects "trial" your offering, offer samples of output based on their specific requirements. You control the output and can manage their expectations much better than if they were given free reign to access the product.

If what you are offering can't stand up to either of these tests of usability or quality, you shouldn't be selling it. You are too good of a salesperson to waste your time on inferior offerings; find a company that offers or does something you can sell with pride.

There is an alternative approach that is a little too close to a free trial for our comfort, but you might find it works for you.

We call these "structured evaluations." A free trial implies an unstructured, no-holds-barred, try-to-break-the-damn-thing approach to evaluating a product.

A structured evaluation is similar in that you are providing access to a product for the prospect without any underlying contractual agreement, but that is where the similarity ends.

**WITH A STRUCTURED EVALUATION:**

- You (the salesperson) agree with the client on what will be evaluated, and what the barometers of success for that evaluation will be.

- The salesperson clarifies all commercial terms with the client.

- The client agrees that if those barometers of success are achieved, she will purchase the product at the commercial terms they've been given.

- The client agrees that if those barometers of success aren't achieved, she will provide feedback on where the breakdown occurred.

- All of this is documented in advance in a two- or three-page structured evaluation document and signed by both parties in advance.

With a structured evaluation, the salesperson is absolutely clear on what is being evaluated, and can orchestrate all his resources to focus on achieving those evaluation criteria. In the unfortunate situation that the product doesn't stand up to the evaluation, at least the salesperson will be given valuable feedback on how to improve the offering to make it more saleable. If the evaluation meets all the criteria, the sale has already been agreed on and it's just an administrative matter of moving the formal paperwork from the structured evaluation document to a formal contract.

If you want to give something away, forget the "trial" part and just give it away. Do it as a show of solidarity and partnership. Do it as you would to a close friend who asks to borrow a $1000. Only lend him as much as you can afford to not have paid back. Do it out of a commitment to a long-term relationship with specific goals in mind, but be enough of a realist to know that you might never see your $1000 again.

> *You are too good of a salesperson to waste your time on inferior offerings; find a company that offers or does something you can sell with pride.*

---

### NEGOTIATION

A man walks up to a beautiful woman in a bar and says, "If I gave you a million dollars would you sleep with me?"

She thinks about it for a moment, looks him up and down, narrows her eyes and pouts her lips and says, "Yes."

He says, "Would you for $100?"

Indignant, she growls out, "What do you take me for?"

Smiling, the man says, "We have already determined that and now we are just negotiating the price."

### Son's Story
### THANK YOU FOR SMOKING

The Philip Morris receptionist in Tokyo is extremely beautiful and the waiting area, decorated with exotic plants and plush white leather sofas, is elegant. And very, very smoky. On the reception counter a large sign reads "Thank you for smoking." There is the ubiquitous no-smoking sign, a cigarette with a red line through it, except there is no red line. Several salespeople like me are waiting in the reception area. And they are all smoking Marlboro—indoors—taken directly from the many containers scattered around the room filled with free packs of Marlboro Reds, Lights, Menthols, and Virginia Slims for the ladies.

Philip Morris, the largest tobacco company in the world, was a powerhouse in the heavy-smoking nation of Japan circa the year 2000, equaled only by national incumbent Japan Tobacco. They were undertaking a customer service initiative that involved printing a phone number on every pack of cigarettes so that their customers could reach a call center and comment on the product. The Japanese are notorious perfectionists, even about their cigarettes, and Philip Morris expected call volume to be massive and needed to build a state-of-the-art call center to accommodate.

I was 26 and had been a salesperson for less than a year; I was there to meet the CIO (chief information officer) as one of the two companies chosen to compete for this massive multimillion-dollar project.

Backtrack a few months. I was at a networking event in Tokyo. A get-together for IT professionals where you drank beer and glad-handled everyone in the room while passing

## Secret #2: "FREE TRIALS" ARE FOR LOSERS

out business cards. About 80 percent of the attendees were headhunters, financial planners, and salespeople like me. A sparse 20 percent were IT professionals. One of the many people I met was a friendly Australian guy named Martin.

Me: Hi, I'm Brian, what do you do?
Martin: I run IT for Philip Morris.
Me: Really? You need any routers?

Now I don't recommend this straightforward approach unless you are young and dumb and three beers into a 10-beer night. Fortunately Martin took me at face value.

Martin: Actually I do. I've been asking all of my vendors for a Cisco 1730 router, just a little tiny thing. We want to do some tests and I just need it for a couple of weeks so I don't want to buy it.
Me: Understood, I'll look in to it.

I wandered off to find pretty girl headhunters to flirt with and Martin probably figured he'd seen the last of me.

The next day in the office I found the head of our infrastructure group and asked him if he had any 1730 routers. He asked me why I wanted that little thing and I said I needed it for a prospect as a show of goodwill. He reached under his desk and pulled out this tiny little router and handed it to me and said I could use it for a couple of weeks. I took it and went back to my desk and checked the price. It cost around $1000 and I decided that was $1000 I was willing to part with.

I called Martin and he was pretty surprised to hear from me. I told him I had his router and asked who I should deliver it to. He asked me how much. I told him it was free; I was giving it to him. We had a spare lying around and he could use it for as long as he wanted. If he didn't need it anymore he could give it back to me.

Two hours later I was standing in his office handing

the router over to his top guy. So now I was personally connected with the head of IT, and his top lieutenant.

After that gesture of goodwill, Martin was happy to take a meeting the following week, where I went in with product experts from my side and learned about the call center plans.

We had a strong team and were well prepared to deliver a compelling presentation on our capabilities in the space, and were ultimately one of only two companies invited to participate in the bid.

We won the deal; I got my sale and first big client. I got a huge commission check and, then in an annual Cisco awards ceremony, was awarded "Best Call Center Deal" for the year, and presented with a trophy and $5000 by a Japanese television celebrity. I split the 5000 bucks with my tech guys and took them out for drinks and they never asked for the router back.

I became personal friends with Martin and was frequently invited to parties at his home, where I met other great prospects and built my business network in Tokyo.

I was also very popular in the office because I got in the habit of remembering what my colleagues smoked and grabbing a few packs every time I went to Philip Morris.

The power of giving.

# Secret #3

## OVERPREPARE FOR EVERY MEETING

### (PRIOR PREPARATION PREVENTS PISS-POOR PERFORMANCE)

*There are no shortcuts to proper meeting preparation. Your preparation lets you tailor the meeting to your prospect's interests and needs, distinguishing the great salesperson from the merely average.*

One of my sales managers had a saying that got more annoying each time he said it (at least three times a day—for *four years*). "Prior Preparation Prevents Piss-Poor Performance." Annoying but true.

How do you prepare for client meetings, and how long does it take you?

Do any of the following describe you?

- Jotting down talking points for the meeting on the subway or cab on the way to the meeting

- Getting lost on the way to the meeting

- Sweating heavily from your brisk run to get to the meeting almost (but not quite) on time

- Showing up 12 minutes late for the meeting

- Unable to tell the receptionist which department the person you are visiting is in when she asks

- Using your phone for talking or texting when your client walks into the meeting room

- Starting the meeting with "Just wanted to catch up!" or "How's business?"

- Losing your pen or forgetting to bring a notepad

- Looking at the client's business card during meeting to remember his name

If selling is important to you (Translation: If you care about being successful and making money), shouldn't you approach every single meeting as if it will define your future relationship with that client?

## Secret #3: OVERPREPARE FOR EVERY MEETING
### (PRIOR PREPARATION PREVENTS PISS-POOR PERFORMANCE)

Because every meeting does.

Did it sound a little revolutionary when we told you that getting on email twice a day is plenty?

Actually it wasn't revolutionary, it was old-fashioned.

Call your clients. Meet your clients. Interact with them meaningfully so that they remember you. Study them and study their business. Articulate your offering in context with what you have learned about them, and every sale will be unique, meaningful, and beget further sales as you evolve into a trusted partner.

Selling is important to you. You want to be successful at it. Your clients are important to you. You want to make money. Because all of these things are true (and here is where we are going to sound pretty old-fashioned again) you should be spending two hours preparing for each and every client meeting.

You should be walking into that meeting having absolutely exhausted every possible source of information about that client and his company. You have spent significant time studying him personally, planning what you will discuss, thinking about which of your offerings might be relevant to him. You have orchestrated your internal teams in strategy sessions to fully tap your company's communal brain.

You will walk into that meeting fully armed with everything you or anyone else involved in the meeting can think of.

The power of overpreparing for every meeting comes from the confidence you develop through the overpreparation. If you have done 90 minutes of research on the company and 30 minutes of research on the person with whom you are meeting, and have three stories and two jokes in your back pocket, you are going to feel pretty confident walking into a meeting with anyone.

You aren't going to need everything that you know, but you are going to know everything that you need.

> *If selling is important to you (Translation: If you care about being successful and making money), shouldn't you approach every single meeting as if it will define your future relationship with that client?*

## CONTEXTUAL COVERAGE

By contextual coverage, we mean that you are interacting with your client contextually based on what you found out about him before you met, and then tweaking that interaction based on what you learn about him while you interact. This can happen in real time (e.g. during an actual meeting). Or it can be more medium to long term. For example, you have a meeting and go back and digest and brainstorm, and then re-engage with an even more tailored and relevant approach based on what you learned previously.

Think of a salesperson as a jazz musician. First you learn all the scales and chords and how to play classical music. Once you've mastered all the underlying principles and have all the information you need, you put it in your back pocket and forget about it. You go out on stage and listen to your bandmates play, you watch the audience, you listen to the silences between the notes, and you improvise.

## Secret #3: OVERPREPARE FOR EVERY MEETING
### (PRIOR PREPARATION PREVENTS PISS-POOR PERFORMANCE)

This is a concept that's easy to screw up.

Improvisation is not spur-of-the-moment, random acts generated without deep thought. The ability to improvise comes from putting in the time with the basic principles and owning them as your own.

**THREE STEPS TO MASTERY THAT APPLY TO ANY DISCIPLINE:**

1. **BEGINNER**—follow the rules
2. **INTERMEDIATE**—test the rules
3. **MASTER**—create your own rules

You should never walk into a meeting with a client as a "beginner." You should already have studied the rules. The meeting is your chance to test them. You will engage with your client in "context" and you will cover him in the future "contextually," within the frame of your past meaningful interactions and your increasing understanding of his needs.

**OVERPREPARATION FOR A MEETING MIGHT INCLUDE:**

- **SCOURING THE INTERNET FOR INFORMATION ABOUT THE COMPANY**
  Don't just read "About" and "News" pages, check the "Hiring" section as well. It can give you valuable hints about the company's current initiatives and focus.

- **SCOURING THE INTERNET FOR INFORMATION ABOUT THE CLIENT**
  Where did he go to school? Where did he work

previously? Does he have any unique personal interests or hobbies?

- **USING YOUR PERSONAL/BUSINESS NETWORK**
  Do you have any acquaintances in common who you could call and ask, "Hey, I'm meeting Ross next week, what kind of guy is he?" Keep it light, you're not stalking Ross, you're looking for basic personality traits here. Is he easygoing, intolerant of bullshit, on the way up, or has his star already risen?

- **USING SOCIAL MEDIA**
  There is an absurd amount of information available online through friends of friends of friends and their respective links and photo walls. You already know how to use this stuff. Comment on "appropriate" topics (ones your human resources manager would approve of).

  Don't be creepy about it.

  > **APPROPRIATE**: I was looking at your Facebook page and saw that you run triathlons. I was thinking of getting into that, do you train with a local group?

  > **CREEPY**: So, I see that your daughter is graduating from U of Penn this year. Where do your other kids go to school?

Secret #3: **OVERPREPARE FOR EVERY MEETING**
(PRIOR PREPARATION PREVENTS PISS-POOR PERFORMANCE)

- **USING ANY INTERNAL TOOLS AVAILABLE**
  You might have access to a CRM (client relationship management) system that is filled with a wealth of historical information about who met this client before and what they talked about. Print this out, read it, and then read it again. Be prepared to say the client's own words back to him. He may not remember saying it, but will be impressed when his thoughts are coming out of your mouth.

- **USING YOUR COLLEAGUES**
  Have a meaningful human interaction with any of your colleagues who might be able to help you make this a meaningful interaction with your client. Your CRM tells you that Tony, who works in marketing, met Ross before. Walk over to Tony's desk and tell him what you have learned about Ross so far, and what your goal is (this demonstrates your seriousness about working with Ross so that Tony gets serious about helping you). Tony can give you valuable contextual information based on his past interactions with Ross.

- **TAILORING YOUR PRESENTATION**
  If what you sell is something that has an element of customization, customize as much as you reasonably can in line with what you think Ross might like (note that you are at the "intermediate" level here, testing the rules). Something as simple as Ross' company's logo on a handout shows that you thought and cared about the meeting. Something

more time intensive sends an even more powerful message.

You are rarely, probably never, going to use all this research in your meeting. In fact, you're going to probably use 10 percent or less of it. Overprepare so that nothing will surprise you, and you can quickly ascertain the deeper subtext of what is being said during the meeting. Imagine the feeling of confidence you'll have walking into a meeting with someone you have never met, yet knowing where he went to college, what he majored in, and what his last three jobs were. And because you spoke to his racquetball buddy on the phone last night, you know where he vacations and exactly what he ate for lunch yesterday. Empowering to say the least.

---

### CUSTOMIZING YOUR CHAT

There was a young Japanese life insurance salesman who used to call on me. Each time we met, his version of an opening icebreaker was to tell me about some interesting bit of news like, "Did you hear about this new kind of Gortex that is rainproof and can even stand up to attack by a bear's claw?" Literally, that was something he told me. It was weird, but rather interesting, and I found it endearing that he went to the trouble of preparing animal attack stories to entertain me.

His insurance offering might not have been the best, but I liked him and he concluded a successful sales engagement with me.

Secret #3: OVERPREPARE FOR EVERY MEETING
(PRIOR PREPARATION PREVENTS PISS-POOR PERFORMANCE)

## LESS IS MORE

You or your team might have spent hours preparing an incredible presentation with graphics and compelling charts, complete with the client's logo all over it and revolutionary ideas that you think could change his business. Just because a lot of time was spent creating that presentation, you do not have to use it if it doesn't fit into the discussion that develops during the meeting.

Maybe Ross will tell you something during the meeting and you will realize that what you've prepared misses the mark entirely. Or maybe he'll tell you something so significant that making a few slight changes to what you've already prepared will dramatically improve it. Be patient and don't offer anything that isn't relevant. In other words, only offer the most relevant pieces of what you prepared. You might have a 20-page document prepared but end up using only one page—the page that you know is going to have the profoundest effect on Ross based on what you've learned so far in the meeting.

There's nothing worse than an unseasoned salesperson pulling out a slide deck and saying, "I know that you just told me you aren't interested in widgets, but I prepared this 20-page document on widgets and was hoping to run you through it." You either keep the stupid document in your folder, or you pull out page 20, the one that says, "Just in Case You Don't Like Widgets," and you focus on that.

Doing all of this preparation diligently will take some time. That's okay. You have freed up so much time by eliminating mindless email from your daily tasks that you now have the time to focus exclusively on preparing to call or meet your clients, and then actually calling and meeting them.

It might take you two to three hours to overprepare. That's just your part. You might have a team of three that spends a couple of hours customizing something for the client. There are an enormous amount of resources that went into this client meeting in an effort to make it meaningful.

So why two hours?

Well, at least an hour to research and prepare, define your agenda, rehearse your line of questioning and talking points. Then an hour for the meeting itself. (There is nothing wrong with a 15- or 30-minute meeting as long as it is meaningful.) You will also be spending some time on follow-up.

> There's nothing worse than an unseasoned salesperson pulling out a slide deck and saying, "I know that you just told me you aren't interested in widgets, but I prepared this 20-page document on widgets and was hoping to run you through it."

You spent all this time preparing for the meeting personally. Your colleagues spent time helping you prepare. There has been a huge investment in resources and brainpower. Don't waste it.

## THE FOLLOW-UP

What distinguishes a great salesperson from an amateur is the follow-up.

Secret #3: OVERPREPARE FOR EVERY MEETING
(PRIOR PREPARATION PREVENTS PISS-POOR PERFORMANCE)

## THREE KEY ELEMENTS TO THE FOLLOW-UP:

1. Express thanks for the opportunity to have a meeting
2. Note the most important points that came out of the meeting (prove you were listening)
3. Lay the groundwork for the next meeting

A "meeting" doesn't have to be a formal meeting, just a two-sided interaction that is meaningful. It might be a phone call or a chance meeting in a bar.

An email is not an engagement. An email is a one-sided communication that might become two-sided at some unidentifiable time in the future. When? When you receive a reply. If you receive a reply. Who replies to email these days unless it's their boss, lover, or best friend? And out of those three, boss is definitely lowest priority, right? Who has time to reply to email if they are only checking email a couple of minutes every day and single mindedly focusing on meaningful human interactions? Not your prospect. Not you.

The follow-up itself can be carried out through an email, as a one-sided communication. Fine in this case. You are saying thank you and telling your prospect what you are going to do next, and don't need to sit around waiting for a "you're welcome" to get started on that. The follow-up is simply setting the stage for the next meeting.

Ideally, the follow-up happens within 24 hours of the engagement. If there is something time intensive that needs to be prepared for the prospect as part of the follow-up, you should still follow up within 24 hours to note that you are working on what was discussed, and when you expect to have it ready.

## FOLLOW-UP EMAIL EXAMPLE

> Ross,
>
> Thank you for your time and the frank discussion yesterday. Now that I have a better understanding of where specifically you are looking to originate new deals (Southeast Asia, chiefly in the industrial and real estate sector), I'll have the team put together a few sample reports around that as discussed. I will send that over to you by next Wednesday, and will follow up with a call to walk you through it.
>
> Regards,
> Brian

- Expressing thanks and noting that the discussion was real and true ("frank")

- Recalling the most important details of the meeting: Facts that came out of the meeting, in this case what (originating new deals in two specific sectors) and where (Southeast Asia), and telling Ross what/when for the next step

- Confirming your intention to remain engaged and setting the groundwork for the next meaningful human interaction

Follow these simple rules for the follow-up. This alone will make you better than 90 percent of the salespeople

*What distinguishes a great salesperson from an amateur is the follow-up.*

## Secret #3: OVERPREPARE FOR EVERY MEETING
### (PRIOR PREPARATION PREVENTS PISS-POOR PERFORMANCE)

out there, and you will impress your prospects and clients with your attention to detail and commitment to their business.

## WHEN YOU DON'T HAVE TWO HOURS

The best-laid plans can go awry. You worked all day until 6 p.m., then caught a flight to the airport, hopped on a plane for a four-hour ride, during which you frantically finished a proposal due before tomorrow, and ended up checking into your hotel at your destination after midnight. You don't have the energy to order a shitty club sandwich from room service, let alone prep for tomorrow's 9 a.m. meeting.

Don't make this a habit, but here's a way to do an abbreviated prep in about 30 minutes.

Wake up as early as you can drag yourself out of bed. Make a quick list of what you would ideally prep for the 9 a.m. meeting. It might look like this:

- Research person I'm meeting
- Study his company
- Study his business unit
- Understand his competitive landscape
- Key questions to ask

Now, define your goal for the meeting in one sentence.

For example: Confirm Ross' main region of interest as head of overseas strategy, and how he measures his success in that region.

Out of those five prep points that you listed, identify the one that is going to give you the biggest bang for the buck as it relates to your specific meeting goal, and spend 20 minutes thinking about and researching that topic.

In this case, it's probably going to be "understand his competitive landscape" so that you'll walk into the meeting ready to test some assumptions about what his main focus is as head of overseas strategy, and how he would define success related to his competitors. Spend the final 10 minutes outlining the meeting agenda in a few bullet points and thinking of a few intelligent questions.

Asking the right questions is the second most important thing in any meeting.

The most important thing? Really listening to the answers.

With this 30-minute prep you'll walk into that meeting with a tight agenda, some thoughtful questions, and high-level understanding of Ross' competitive landscape. This presumes that you are well versed in pitching your own solution, and don't need to prep that. It's not ideal as your preparation is too generic to be really great, but it will get you through the meeting without embarrassment.

Remember, this is the fix-it-with-rubber-bands-and-glue approach and should be used sparingly.

## WHEN YOU DON'T HAVE 30 MINUTES

Get on the phone and call the smartest person in your organization or personal network and say, "I'm meeting with Ross in 15 minutes, what kind of questions should I ask him?"

This has saved me more than once. It's amazing how

## Secret #3: OVERPREPARE FOR EVERY MEETING
### (PRIOR PREPARATION PREVENTS PISS-POOR PERFORMANCE)

thoughtful questions can demonstrate an understanding of your prospect's business. Asking the right questions will get him talking and help make up for your lack of prep, as he tells you everything you wanted to know.

Thoughtful questions make the meeting.

---

*Asking the right questions is the second most important thing in any meeting. The most important thing? Really listening to the answers.*

---

### Son's Story
### THAT DESERTED ISLAND THING

One of the hardest sales calls I've had to make was to the CEO of a company that used to employ me. I had been their top performing salesperson in Japan and was well acquainted with their senior management. I had left that company five or six years prior and had little contact with anyone from there since.

I was in the business then of management consulting (selling ideas, no product to show), and wanted to take my offering to Bill, the CEO at the company.

Reconnecting with Bill and arranging to meet him during my next business trip to Singapore was easy. We traded emails and spoke on the phone and he was happy to meet. But he was happy to meet because of our previous relationship, not necessarily because he was a buyer for my firm's consulting services.

So a few things were going on here for me. One was that I needed to understand Bill's current state of affairs. I had remained friendly with his head of marketing and arranged a dinner with her the night before my Bill meeting. She would tell me whatever non-confidential information I asked about the business and I was reassured that I would be up to speed on what was relevant to them.

The other thing that was going on for me was that I had a reputation to uphold. I had been one of Bill's top sales guys seven years ago. There was a certain amount of personal pride invested in being my best self in this meeting. I spent an entire weekend crafting my pitch and a meaningful slide deck, and then I role-played the meeting twice, having my colleague play a very tough Bill. By the second role-play

## Secret #3: OVERPREPARE FOR EVERY MEETING
### (PRIOR PREPARATION PREVENTS PISS-POOR PERFORMANCE)

I felt like my game was on point. I was ready to pitch Bill.

At this point, I had invested way more than five hours in preparation. In fact I was much closer to 20.

There was still something else I needed though. I felt that I needed some stories or anecdotes that I could call on to demonstrate a point, or just to pull out if Bill didn't seem like he was ready to be pitched. I thought hard about this and ultimately chose two anecdotes that I thought would get Bill's attention. I wrote both the stories out and edited them perfectly. By the time I was done, I had virtually committed them to memory. I was ready to go to Singapore.

Bill, CEO of thousands, walked into the room in a casual shirt and jeans and was super relaxed and friendly. We caught up for 15 minutes until he asked the question: "So, what did you come here to sell me?"

Some of you reading this book have been asked that question. It's a killer. The answer is never "nothing," and using that to segue into your sales pitch might not feel quite right. You need to make a split-second decision about what to do with that question. Does the client genuinely want to hear the pitch? Do they just want you to get on with it so that they can hear you out and send you on your way?

I had spent a lot of time, 20 hours plus, thinking about Bill, getting reacquainted with his business, role-playing different possible outcomes for the meeting. My split-second decision based on all that preparation was that Bill wasn't ready to hear the pitch. If I had pulled out my slide deck and overwhelmed him with a bunch of logic, he may have been impressed, but I wasn't sure that would have made him a buyer.

I sensed that Bill needed to feel it in his bones, so I told him a story.

You are on a boat. A big boat. The *Titanic*. You are on the *Titanic*, and it runs into some rocks and starts to sink.

You jump in a lifeboat, all alone, and are washed up on a deserted island.

What is the first thing that you do?

The answer that you will get here is invariably one of three things: "Search for food," "Search for water," "Find shelter."

That's what most people say. However, what we've found is that those who take a very strategic view towards leadership answer differently.

What those leaders say they will do first is find the highest point on the island and climb to the very top.

When you are at the top of the tallest tree on the island, you will see where the food is.

When you are at the top of the highest hill on the island, you will see where the water is.

When you are at the highest point on the island you can look at across the sea and see the pirates coming your way. If you can see the pirates when they are four days out, you can plan for their arrival. What would happen if you only notice them when they are four minutes out?

Seeing the pirates when they are four days out is the same as seeing the future.

How do you climb to the highest place on the island? Don't you need special shoes, hiking gear, other capabilities that you don't have?

This is where my company comes in. We partner with you to decide the kind of gear you need. We help you look at your capabilities and

## Secret #3: OVERPREPARE FOR EVERY MEETING
### (PRIOR PREPARATION PREVENTS PISS-POOR PERFORMANCE)

decide if you need new ones to make the ascent. We walk up to the top with you, and we talk about what you see, and out of that dialogue comes new realizations and actions.

What would you do next once you've reached that highest point?

The true leader will find somewhere higher. He'll build an airplane so that he can see all the deserted islands around him. He'll build a spaceship so that he can go even higher and see the continents and the great oceans in between.

So you're on a boat, a huge boat, and it runs into a bunch of rocks and you end up on a deserted island.

What do you do first?

A colleague had joined me for the meeting and when we were in the taxi afterwards I asked him for some feedback on how he thought it went. "That story you told was the turning point," he said to me. "It's like that story opened up Bill's ears to what you had to say."

The next day, Bill's head of HR (human resources) called to ask me to come in for a meeting with the head of sales to talk about our "deserted island thing." From that one-hour meeting, the one thing that had really stuck with Bill was that story.

That meeting with the heads of HR and sales turned into several more, and my ex-employer became my biggest client over the subsequent years.

# Secret #4

## SHUT UP AND LISTEN

*Stop talking so much, start listening more, and let your client tell you exactly what he wants. Then sell it to him.*

Ever heard the phrase "two ears, one mouth"? It means that human beings have twice the number of ears as mouths, so we should spend twice as much time listening as talking.

Shutting your mouth is one of the most important skills you should master for sales and for life. It sounds easier than it is, and there is an element of psychology here. Long silences in a conversation feel awkward, especially during a one-on-one conversation. People rush to fill those pauses with meaningless words to avoid the awkwardness.

This is a truth you can test out easily on the next three people you talk to today. Keep your answers monosyllabic and count to 10 in your head every time you say something. You'll never reach 10 because the other person will start to talk. If they ask a question, count to 10 before you answer. You'll never reach 10 because they will repeat the question or rephrase it, misinterpreting your silence for misunderstanding. Ten seconds of silence feels like five times that in a one-on-one conversation.

You'll quickly notice that the less you talk, the more the other person talks. This is good. The clever salesperson wants his clients talking. He wants them to tell him exactly how he should be selling to them because then all he has to do is follow the guidelines they lay out for him to achieve a successful sale. (We want a happy buyer *and* happy seller.)

When someone says, "He's such a great conversationalist," what he means is, "I talked way too much and he was such a great listener."

*Shutting your mouth is one of the most important skills you should master for sales and for life.*

Try this in a bar. Approach a member of the opposite sex and open the conversation with something about that person and keep the conversation about him or her by asking leading questions and employing the 10-second rule of silence. Guys, this is how you pick up girls in case you hadn't figured it out yet. In a three- to five-minute conversation, it's amazing how much you can learn about someone by asking gently prodding questions and shutting up.

The other great thing about shutting up is that it gives you time to think before the words come shooting out of your mouth. This is especially important when you are selling complex solutions or services (We're not selling hamburgers here, right?). Sophisticated conversations require thought, and often during a meeting you will be taking in massive amounts of new information. Giving yourself moments of silence to process it is just common sense.

Shutting up is way harder to do in practice than it sounds. Here are some beginner's tips:

- Practice the 10-second rule in your personal life before taking it to meetings; use it on your family members and friends, and play with extending to longer silences of 20 seconds or more without appearing to ignore the person or to be rude.

- Use body language while you are shutting up: nod your head, keep your palms open and displayed in the universal gesture of "Please continue, tell me more." (There is a whole chapter on the important subject of body language coming up.)

- When you first start to employ silence in a business setting you will find it extremely awkward. One trick is to look down and take notes on your notepad, even if they are just gibberish, while you wait for the other person to continue talking.

---

*When someone says, "He's such a great conversationalist," what he means is, "I talked way too much and he was such a great listener."*

---

Secret #4: **SHUT UP AND LISTEN**

### Son's Story
### BLACK BELT IN SILENCE

I learned silence on the job from one of my mentors in sales. He was the global head of sales based in New York, while I ran sales for the Asia region, based in Hong Kong. For the first 12 months of our relationship we never met in person, and all of our interactions were done over the phone. We had a regular weekly call that was scheduled for 6 p.m. NYC time, which was 6 a.m. for me in Hong Kong.

I thought this guy was pretty weird. We'd talk for about an hour each time, 15 minutes of which were filled with silence.

He'd ask me a question and I'd answer. And then there'd be nothing but static on the line for what felt like minutes until I either started talking again, repeating myself in mindless repetition, or started asking the phone, "Hey, can you hear me, are you still there?" It was six in the morning for me, and I was eager to end the call and start my day. I didn't have a lot of patience for these long pauses. What salesperson wants to talk to his boss for an hour at six in the morning?

I spoke to my other colleagues in sales around the world and they all said the same thing about phone calls with him. Long silences during calls. We came to the conclusion that he was reading his emails while he talked to us, and wrote it off as eccentric behavior.

Then he came out to see me and I realized that I had it all wrong. He was a black belt in silence.

We had client meetings together and he would just stop talking. In the beginning, not knowing any better, I would start in with mindless chatter, anything to fill the silences that felt extremely awkward to me.

After a couple of meetings like that he said, "When I stop talking, don't talk."

That was as much of a hint as I ever got from him that what he was doing was absolutely intentional, but it was enough.

We were in Japan together during his trip and the meetings were with Japanese clients, a reticent group culturally. I vividly remember a meeting with Manabe-san, a managing director at a massive Japanese conglomerate who ran the team tasked with acquiring other companies. An important job to say the least.

Manabe was smooth. Silver-haired, immaculate suit, and he spoke absolutely impeccable English. What I didn't know was that Manabe himself was a master of silence.

During the meeting, my mentor was his usual self, extremely overprepared, and the conversation was going well. Then there was a moment when he wanted to know more and went to his usual silence, head nodding, palms openly displayed, encouraging Manabe to go on. The thing was, Manabe didn't want to tell him more. These two had full penetrating eye contact, neither of them talking for, I swear, what must have been 90 seconds.

It was beyond awkward. I couldn't take it and had to look down to my notepad and start writing. I was writing "long awkward silence, this is weird."

The person that Manabe had brought with him was as visibly discomfited as I, and was also looking down. The longest silence in the history of a meeting ended when Manabe looked at me, smiled widely, and then looked back to my boss and started talking again. It was like two swordsmen facing off with swords undrawn until one bows politely and goes on his way. The fight was decided and didn't require bloodshed to prove the outcome.

## Secret #4: SHUT UP AND LISTEN

Afterwards, I told my boss that had been possibly the most awkward moment I had ever had in a meeting, and he said to me, "I loved it."

This was one of the most valuable lessons I've had in my career in sales, and was the genesis of my decision to master the art of silence.

The 6 a.m. calls went on once my boss headed back to New York. Now though, to stop myself from talking, I jammed a pen in my mouth, bit down on it hard, and shut the hell up. I knew I had made it when one day my boss asked me, "Hey, you still there?"

Once I had mastered the principal of shutting up I began to teach it to the salespeople on my team. In a nod to that epic moment with Manabe in Japan, I awarded them different degrees of colored belts, as in karate, when they demonstrated silence effectively in role-plays and client meetings.

### Dad's Story
### BARRY CAN'T STOP TALKING

Barry was a highly educated salesperson who had graduated from a respected Ivy League school. To say he was articulate would be an understatement. His language was crisp, rapid, and precise. He used words that most people would have to look up in the dictionary (well, at least I had to look up some of the words he used). He loved to talk because he loved to hear himself. I did not hire Barry. He came with the staff that I inherited when I took the job. He interested me and I liked him, although he was the brunt of every other salesperson's jokes because of his use of $100 words. The teasing didn't faze him though, he continued to talk. And boy could Barry talk.

In our internal sales meetings he would ask questions like, "If the prospect doesn't perceive the abhorrent consequences of sustaining their current pattern of behavior, how can we be charged with alleviating his downward spiral towards a predictable outcome?" Yeah, exactly.

One afternoon I sat down with Barry and told him that it was more important to listen to what his customers said than listen to his own voice. Barry had thick skin and he did not bat an eye, commenting that many of his clients just like to hear their own voices. This, from Barry?

"Barry," I said, "You are not going to make it in sales unless you learn to keep your mouth shut. Your perceptions are usually very valid, and you can give your recommendations, but do not try to tell your client how to run his business." Barry was smart, and he agreed that he would try to tone it down.

## Secret #4: **SHUT UP AND LISTEN**

A week or so later my assistant told me that Barry was working on a proposal for a client that included a comprehensive ad campaign for all of their television stations in the market. In the proposal he had even included staff training. And guess who he had volunteered to run the training? Me.

I told my assistant to take everything out of the proposal except his plan for the one station where we had scheduled a meeting. Absolutely no staff training. The presentation was set for the following day.

I told Barry that I would join him on the sales call, and we set out to meet the client. He presented the proposal and it went very well. The client said he thought it would work and thanked Barry for his insights and recommendations. The sale was as good as closed, and it would be a very lucrative contract.

But, Barry kept talking.

He started in on the other stations and what we could do for them. I recalled the conversation with my assistant and could guess what was coming next. He was going to tell them how great of a trainer I was and offer up that service as well. This was not our goal for the meeting.

The goal for the meeting was to walk out of there with a commitment to the one thing that we were offering in our proposal, and then leverage that sale to build credibility and expand our business with the client.

I kicked him under the table before this went too far and he let out a suppressed squeal. His eyes teared up slightly and the client was looking at him strangely, but—to his benefit—he recovered quickly and said that he was suffering a leg cramp because of a low-carb diet and was sorely lacking in potassium. That was Barry for you. Anyway, he got the message and shut up and we walked out of there with a signed deal.

We got in the car to head back to the office and he showed me where I had kicked him and it had swollen up to the size of a tennis ball. I was horrified. Apparently I had nailed him right on the edge of his shin bone and, although I hadn't kicked him that hard, the pain was excruciating and he had a lump there for two weeks.

Years later he told me that kick had made such an impact that he never forgot to shut up when he knew he had the sale.

# Secret #5

## MASTER BODY LANGUAGE

*Skillful salespeople can read and interpret both the verbal and the nonverbal ways their clients communicate. Uncross your arms, sit up straight, and let's talk about what the body is saying.*

Once you begin to use silence effectively, you'll naturally start to employ nonverbal means of communicating, otherwise known as body language. Reading body language is one of the most neglected sales skills, yet it will tremendously impact your ability to sell.

Body language is so important that you should read several books on it. You should practice to the point that when you walk into a party filled with people, within a few minutes you can identify the relationships between all the people in the room. You should be able to observe a couple in a coffee shop and quickly discern if they are relatives, friends, or lovers. And more specifically for the salesperson, reading body language during a meeting with a prospect will dramatically improve your timing on when to ask for the sale, and measurably increase your ability to sell.

We study salespeople, and what we've come to know is that the greatest of them intuitively or intentionally use very specific body language and are experts in reading others. Studies show that more than 90 percent of human communication is nonverbal. The way you walk is more important than the way you talk.

We recommend you start with an overview, something like *The Definitive Guide to Body Language* by Barbara Pease. Then once you have a general understanding of the basics, you can dive deeper into the nuances of what will benefit you most. Negotiation skills for example, essential for great salespeople, are in large part linked to the ability to read body language.

This is not about being manipulative to get what you want. It is about presenting what you are offering in the best possible way, when the person you are presenting to is in the best possible mindset to receive it. Perhaps you could consider this as "tailor-making" your communication for your client.

Here are some of the techniques that will give you the biggest bang for your buck.

## UNCROSS THE ARMS

Never ask for a sale when your prospect's arms are crossed. This is the most important body language skill to learn right away. Crossed arms represent a disapproving or negative mindset. Your prospect,

### Secret #5: MASTER BODY LANGUAGE

regardless of what he is telling you, is not convinced. You need to do or say something that will open his arms and make him more receptive to what you are offering.

Studies on university students have shown repeatedly that crossed arms during a lecture *decrease* the amount of information retained by as much as 50 percent. Your prospect with the crossed arms not only dislikes what you are saying, he won't even remember what you said later!

Start catching yourself when you go to cross your own arms. Start this as soon as you put this book down. Do you do it several times a day, habitually? Does it feel comfortable? If your mood is often negative or disapproving, of course it will feel comfortable. The inverse of the university studies is also true—keeping the arms open dramatically increases the ability to retain information. Want to really learn something? Approach it with an open mind and uncrossed arms.

Unless you intentionally want to broadcast a negative attitude, *never* cross your arms. We're not talking just work here. Unless you're wearing a T-shirt in Antarctica, never cross your arms in front of your body.

How do you get someone to uncross his or her arms? Ideally you modify what you are saying to something that makes the person feel more positive and he or she will naturally uncross them.

A trickier way of doing this is to offer something to look at and hold, or even something to drink, to coax the arms open.

Another tactic you might employ when you note the arm crossing is to say, "I see you have a question," or "It looks like something is on your mind." Given the ability to voice concerns, the prospect will often naturally uncross his arms. Once the arms are open, he is in a receptive state and it's okay to ask for the sale.

*Start catching yourself when you go to cross your own arms. Start this as soon as you put this book down. Do you do it several times a day, habitually? Does it feel comfortable? If your mood is often negative or disapproving, of course it will feel comfortable.*

## PALMS OPEN

Even more effective at opening crossed arms is when you display your open palms (backs of hands turned down to the ground, palms facing up) along with the "I see you have a question?" technique above. Open palms show nonaggression, and indicate you are being communicative and genuine. Open palms say, "I have nothing to hide," and can put your prospect in a positive frame of mind.

Incidentally for the guys, when a woman displays her wrists and palms to you, as she might when playing with her hair, she likes you. If she does it while she strokes her face, she really likes you. The wrist is a very sensitive area, and a vulnerable one, and her willingness to expose it to you implies trust.

## MIRRORING

Have you ever been in a grumpy mood and someone around you is unbearably cheerful and it drives you crazy? Misery loves company right? This is the basic principle of "mirroring," the practice of matching your body language and words to those of your prospect to elicit a bond.

Human beings naturally mirror each other as a way of bonding and creating rapport. Whether you like someone or not is often decided by whether they move and talk like you.

What happens when you're talking to someone and they yawn? You usually yawn too. This is a DNA hardwired example of mirroring. Human beings mirror each other because from prehistoric times cooperation was beneficial—it resulted in more food and better health for the tribe.

If mirroring sounds odd to you, think of it as "harmonizing" or "pacing." Match your mood, speech patterns, and body language to someone so that they feel comfortable with you. Comfortable because they get a good vibe from someone who acts a lot like them.

### Son's Story
## UNCROSSING THE ARMS

Brittany is very beautiful. She is smiling while she talks to me and appears extremely relaxed. But her arms are crossed over her chest. What's going on?

It's 4 p.m. in Hong Kong and I am calling on a prospective client for the first time. I am in the consulting business, which means that my product is an invisible service, not something that I can put on a table and point out functionality or demonstrate bells and whistles.

Because there is nothing to "show" the prospective client, the sale of consulting services is generated through dialogue—about the client's past and current situation, their desired future state, and my services, which presumably bridge the gap between the "current state" and "desired state." Sales of consulting services require the salesperson to do a lot of strategic questioning and a lot of listening, and have a lot of dialogue.

Back to my meeting with Brittany. Earlier that morning I had facilitated a group training on body language, so I was hypersensitive to body language in all shapes and forms. One of the key points we had spent a lot of time on in that training session was to never ask for a sale when the prospect's arms are crossed.

So I had a very interesting situation here with Brittany. I had met her at a seminar and she asked me to come in to explain my service. Presumably, this was a meeting that she wanted to have. Literally from the moment after she shook my hand though, her arms crossed and I saw a huge disconnect between what her voice and body were saying.

Since I hadn't even said anything yet at this meeting,

here is what I guessed was going on. Brittany was in a very senior position at her company and probably had salespeople calling on her all the time. Your average sales guy is going to go in and start talking about his product and how great it is and he's not going to pay too much attention to what the prospect is saying, so generally it's just an unfulfilling conversation for the prospect. I suspect that, having experienced that multiple times, Brittany was a bit jaded and defensive, expecting me to talk a mile a minute at her.

This is all in hindsight though. At the time, all I had room to register was, *Arms crossed, why? Let's be very gentle here and see if we can get those arms open.*

So what I did for the next 45 minutes or so was to listen. Brittany had a lot to say and I was delighted to be an active listener, sometimes probing with careful questions but mostly, 95 percent of the time, just listening. About 20 minutes into our conversation her arms naturally opened, and they didn't close again for the rest of our meeting.

Interestingly, the point when they opened was when she revealed some very personal ambitions she had within the company. My acknowledgement of that through listening and through my own body language (strong eye contact, nodding, arms/legs uncrossed, palms open) seemed to have been the key that reassured her enough to drop her defensive stance and really open up.

We had a rich conversation where she essentially sold herself on my service. That sale closed in that single meeting, a meeting that could have gone a very different way had I not been attuned to what her body was saying.

Secret #5: **MASTER BODY LANGUAGE**

**Dad's Story
CHARM SCHOOL**

Doug was a handsome young salesperson with an engaging personality. He was a consistent producer, a team player and was generally well liked by his clients. He was predictable and dependable when it came to delivering his quota.

One of Doug's major advertising sales customers was a Toyota dealership. He did well, tracking at about a 30 percent share of the ad spend from that client for well over a year until about six months prior to where this story starts.

Over the past six months, our share of the Toyota business had been dropping a few points every month. By the time of this story it was down to 15 percent or less.

I called his supervisor, our sales manager, into my office and asked what was going on with Doug and Toyota.

"Well, I guess this drop coincides with a new buyer on the account from about six months ago," he told me.

I said that would have been nice to have known because I had a great relationship with the owner of the dealership and I would have made it a point to meet the new buyer.

"Let's set up a lunch with the buyer and make sure Doug can join us," I said. "Also, find out if there is something Doug isn't telling us about this client. I'll call the owner to see if there is a problem."

Doug's sales manager came into my office later that afternoon to report that we had a lunch set up and that he had talked to Doug, who told him there was no issue other than the buyer not being a fan of our programs. Lunch was set for the next day.

Art, the new buyer for Toyota, showed up ten minutes late. No apology and no physical gesture of a greeting. I admit that in the ad sales business this is a little—no, very—unusual. Before he sat down, I stood and offered my hand and thanked him for meeting us on such short notice. His handshake was light and his palm slightly wet. His mannerisms and handshake indicated he might be nervous. I decided to be careful about bringing up his decreased ad expenditures.

When he seated himself, he was rigid and placed his hands in his lap. Then he said, "I knew I was going to have to have this meeting sooner or later. I was expecting it sooner, frankly."

"Art," I replied, "I don't know what you were expecting, but I can assure you we don't have an agenda other than wanting to know what is important to you and the dealership. I am very sorry that I have been so remiss in setting up a lunch with you. No excuses, it's all on me."

He let out a breath and I noticed his shoulders relax. I had placed my hands in my lap and sat up straight and I let out a breath to mirror his behavior.

But this isn't about Art and me; it's about Doug.

During lunch Doug talked with his mouth full, food sometimes spraying out. He wiped his hand on the tablecloth and blew his nose.

On the other hand, Art would not speak with either food in his mouth or a utensil in his hand. He always put his fork down and would speak thoroughly about whatever he was asked and then, and only then, would he resume eating. I mirrored him and, with four people at lunch, he spent 90 percent of the time talking to me even when someone else asked him a question.

On the way back to the office I asked Doug what he thought of the meeting. "Good," he replied. "Art kind of

Secret #5: **MASTER BODY LANGUAGE**

has a stick up his butt, but he seemed cool today."

Back at the office I talked to Doug's sales manager, who said he had never been so embarrassed at a lunch. It was very clear now that Doug was not a good mix with Art and that we had to make a change.

"Who would be a good fit?" I asked.

"Maureen!" the sales manager said enthusiastically. Maureen was a sales assistant who had recently been promoted to salesperson.

Art knew Maureen because of all the work she had done for him on behalf of Doug and said he would love to have her call on him. The turnaround was dramatic and our billing went into the 40 percent range. I personally made it a point to stop and talk with Art when I was at the dealership to see the owner.

Doug did not like losing the account and liked it less when his sales manager suggested he attend charm school. But he did for one night a week for six weeks and he passed with flying colors.

Today Doug is a general manager of a group of television stations; I bet he doesn't give credit to Miss Allie's Charm School.

# Secret #6

## DON'T JUST SELL ONE BANANA (SELL THE WHOLE PLANTATION!)

*Never be in a rush to close a deal.*
*Always have infinite patience to close the right deal.*

### Shanghai, circa 2005

As the top performing salesperson for my company, a pan-Asian IT systems integrator, I was able to leverage relocation from Tokyo to Shanghai. This is a polite way of saying that I told my boss that he could either send me to our Shanghai office for a year or he could have my resignation.

Shanghai was wild—buildings shooting up and getting torn down like a war zone, everybody hustling for a buck. The possibilities seemed limitless. My new sales colleagues in the Shanghai office were making $30,000 a year, but driving around in BMWs, having 12-course Shanghainese cuisine feasts for lunch, and partying at the hottest clubs. Don't ask me where the money was coming from, I'll plead ignorance.

I moved into a nice private condominium complex; a brand new three-bedroom, top-floor condo with marble floors and a maid who came every Saturday to clean the

## Secret #6: DON'T JUST SELL ONE BANANA (SELL THE WHOLE PLANTATION!)

entire house and make me elaborate meals like handmade dumplings. Total price (with the maid): $600 a month. Things were getting more expensive in Shanghai at an exponential rate, but they were still damn cheap.

Each morning when I left my complex to go to work, I passed by a small street vendor who sold fruits. For the first couple of days I stopped to practice my bad Chinese on this guy and buy a banana.

Now, to put this in perspective, the going price for bananas in the supermarket was something like 20 cents per kilogram (around eight bananas, so not quite three cents per banana) so you'd figure this little shop would maybe double the price, sell it to me for five cents or so.

Instead, this guy tried to sell me a banana for 50 cents. I was white and surely had lots of money to burn and wouldn't mind paying almost 20 times what I should pay for a banana. Fair enough, for all he knew, I was a tourist with no sense of the going banana rates.

He was after the transactional sale—no eye contact; happy seller, *unhappy* buyer.

What did he care about my happiness if he was never going to see me again. He had undoubtedly sold many 50-cent bananas to unsuspecting *waiguoren* ("outside people," i.e. non-Chinese) and saw it as a lucrative sales strategy.

This was kind of endearing the first time it happened. We haggled over the banana price and I ultimately had to do the fake walk away and then get called back to get the banana for 10 cents. I would have liked five cents better, but I was still a happy buyer at 10 cents. Sales engagement concluded successfully.

The next day I leave my place and head over to his shop where I expect a friendly greeting and a 10-cent banana. Instead, he tries to charge me 50 cents again. This wasn't so endearing. I thought we had established the previous day that while, yes, I was a fresh-off-the-boat American, I was going to be hanging around for a while, and was intent on buying bananas at the (slightly inflated) local price. So we haggled again as if the previous day hadn't happened, and I ultimately bought the banana for 10 cents.

> **SALES HINT**
> In many Asian cultures, good-natured haggling over the price is the norm. Once an agreement has been reached the seller will often say to the buyer, "You are a great negotiator." True or not, this is an elegant way of complementing the buyer on a successful sales engagement and concluding the sale on a friendly note.

On the third day, he tried to sell me a banana for 50 cents and I flipped him the bird and went to a different fruit stand, where I bought a banana for 5 cents every day for the rest of my stay in China. About 365 bananas.

Don't be shortsighted in your sales strategy. Don't do something silly that will make you a dollar today when you could be smart and make $100 next Tuesday.

That banana vendor should have realized by day three that he had a captive audience for one banana a day at a fair price. If he had been clever, he would have cultivated a friendship with me, complimented me on my poor Chinese and maybe taught me a new word or two, and then gradually—as we had established our steady

## Secret #6: DON'T JUST SELL ONE BANANA (SELL THE WHOLE PLANTATION!)

banana-buying relationship—gone for the upsell: "These bananas are very tasty, but today I have some juicy and sweet Hainan tangerines as well, perhaps you'd like an orange to go with your banana? Or how about a whole box of oranges? I'll give you a very good price since you are such a loyal customer. And your Chinese is improving so quickly, you must be very smart."

Forget about the fruit, this is the kind of thing a buyer wants to hear from a seller in any situation. The seller confirms the successful sales engagement, i.e. you are a happy buyer; I am a happy seller.

*Don't be shortsighted in your sales strategy. Don't do something silly that will make you a dollar today when you could be smart and make $100 next Tuesday.*

Then within that framework of mutual benefit and trust, the seller offers a recommendation for something additional. This "additional" is presented as something that would particularly suit the buyer in this case because of the high quality of the product aligned to the buyer's discerning tastes. And finally the seller offers a special arrangement with an incentive to close the sale.

## UPTICKS

One of our favorite sales strategies is to structure contracts where the price gradually "upticks" over time. This works especially well for sales of complex products with steep learning curves. The client needs to be trained on the product and then practice using it, and it takes some time before the full value of the product is realized, so the contract is structured with that in mind. Start at a low price and move towards a higher price once the product is in mature use within the client's organization.

The philosophy behind upticks is easy to explain to your prospect:

There is a price for this product/service that you will need to pay eventually, that price is not negotiable. I do, however, appreciate that you won't be getting full value right from day one, so what *is* negotiable is when you will start paying full price.

> **SALES HINT**
>
> If your product is something that is regularly enhanced, or something with a pricing model still in flux, be cautious about making the contract too long, as you could be limiting potential upside by locking in the price.

So let's say you are selling something that costs $1 million. The contract with upticks would be structured like this:

**Year 1** - $250K
**Year 2** - $500K
**Year 3** - $1M

Psychologically the buyer is only thinking about the year one and maybe the year two price. Sure they'll have to get budget for the full three-year value of $1.75 million in this case, but they are thinking, *A million bucks is a lot of money, but it's not due until three years from now. Who knows what the company will be like then or what I'll be doing? Three years is a long time, too long to think about...I don't even know what I'm having for lunch today.*

## Secret #6: DON'T JUST SELL ONE BANANA (SELL THE WHOLE PLANTATION!)

This is the psychological secret to those horrible furniture commercials: "NOTHING DOWN! NO PAYMENTS FOR 12 MONTHS!" There is a price, and you will pay it eventually, but don't worry about it for now.

Be careful when structuring a contract with upticks to make sure that the contract cannot be terminated until the full price is reached. If you structure a three-year contract that ultimately upticks the client to the actual price of $1 million, you don't want the client to have an early termination clause after year two. That would be tantamount to discounting your price. An uptick is not a discount, it is a way of recognizing that it may take some time to realize full value, and accommodates the client during that time by charging only a portion of the full price.

An added benefit to the uptick structure is that it incentivizes a long-term agreement. If you are confident in the quality of your offering, then you know that it's to your advantage to make the contract as long as possible. The longer the contract, the more time you and your team have to embed your product into the client's operations. Ideally, you want a situation where your client would never cancel because it would be like getting his legs cut off.

Don't be content getting a good price for one banana today. Get creative in how you structure your agreements; sell a truckload of bananas next month or a banana plantation next year. Always look toward long-term contracts. Even if it means sacrificing some short-term gains, the long-term payoff will be worth it.

## PATIENCE

An old seasoned bull is standing at the top of a mountain, he's moving a bit slow because his joints are achy. He's had a long and illustrious life. He is accompanied by a young bull, strong and fast and ambitious.

The young bull with his keen eyesight spots a heard of attractive cows far down the mountain in the valley. Excited, he says to the old bull, "Look at those beauties! Let's run down this mountain and screw a couple!"

The old bull gives him a long look and a shake of his gray head and says, "Let's walk down this mountain and screw them all."

Secret #6: **DON'T JUST SELL ONE BANANA
(SELL THE WHOLE PLANTATION!)**

**Dad's Story
COOKIES AND PERSISTENCE**

A new account executive just out of college asked me what is the most important trait of a great salesperson. Good question. Not easy to answer. In fact, I always ask sales job candidates that question in interviews, and am fascinated with the variety of answers I get. (Hint: If someone asks you "the most important thing" or "just one thing" in an interview, reply with *one* thing. Not two, three, four, or more.)

There is no right answer here. But I confess that there are a few answers that I like a lot better than others. For example, I am always pleased when one of those interview candidates says, "Listening." Another one I like is "trust," and, in this case, that is how I answered that new salesperson. I told her that trust is the most important thing that she needed to gain from her clients.

Some weeks later she was struggling to close a business deal. We were doing some training on handling objections and she began to go through the "put offs" that she was getting.

Recalling our conversation about trust, I asked her what she was doing to gain her client's trust.

"I see the owner at the dealership every week," she replied.

"Do you just look at him or do you do something?" I asked.

She was puzzled and asked me what I meant. I told her that persistence without substance just makes you a professional visitor. On the other hand, persistence with substance is one of the best ways to gain trust. Always bring your client something that shows that you have been thinking about them and their business—an article, some research pertaining to their industry, or even some cookies with their logo in frosting.

A few months later she signed a long-term agreement with what had been her most difficult prospect. During our weekly sales meeting I asked her to describe the process that got her the contract.

She had "seen" the client every week for 20 weeks with no success. A few months ago, around the time that we had that conversation about persistence versus substance, she had begun to bring him something each time she visited (yes, even cookies with their logo on them). She said the owner finally asked her to come into his office, where he listened to her pitch.

He said he would try her product for a month.

She replied, "I would like to accommodate your request and I can, but I'm afraid that you will not get the results you are after in one month. How about testing it for four months to really give it a chance to work?"

His answer was interesting. "Then I won't have you waiting outside my office for four months, so maybe that's a good idea. Okay, four months, let's just start and see where it goes."

She agreed and continued to bring him relevant materials every week. She didn't have to wait outside his office anymore. Whenever she dropped by—if he was around—he always had a few minutes to chat with her about how the program was doing and review what she had brought him.

After the first month, he agreed to sign up for the rest of the year and increased his budget significantly. The account executive was ecstatic.

"So it worked for you!" she replied.

Secret #6: **DON'T JUST SELL ONE BANANA (SELL THE WHOLE PLANTATION!)**

The owner looked her right in the eyes and said, "I don't know yet, but what I do know is that you will be there for me if I need anything. You have earned my trust and I tell all of my sales guys that if they were only half as persistent as you we'd be the best dealership in five states."

# Secret #7

## YOU ARE NOT A VENDOR

*Good and bad, there are a lot of names that your clients might be calling you on any given day. Carefully customize your offering though, and one label you can always avoid is being called a "vendor."*

You are not a vendor. You are a partner. A partner who looks out for your client's best interests.

We take offense at being called a vendor. What does "vendor" mean? It implies the relationship that a customer has with a vending machine. There are a couple of drinks or snacks being offered and they all cost the same price. Put in some coins, press a button, out comes a snack. If there is a line of people waiting behind you, they will be buying the same snacks for the same price. Repeat, ad infinitum.

Is this the kind of transactional relationship you have with your clients? If it is, put this book down and start looking for a new job—what you are selling now is no different than selling hamburgers at McDonald's. Actually, McDonald's knows this and, behind closed doors, admits they aren't really in the hamburger business:

## Secret #7: YOU ARE NOT A VENDOR

> We are not basically in the food business. We are in the real estate business. The only reason we sell hamburgers is because they are the greatest producer of revenue from which our tenants can pay us rent.
>
> —Harry J. Sonneborn, McDonald's Corp. (MCD) first CFO

You are not a vendor, you are a partner. A partner who looks out for your client's best interests. If you were a vending machine, you'd be one funky vending machine. First of all, the snacks are all highly customizable. The customer can choose the flavor, color, and size. And based on what he chooses, the price is always different. And sometimes it takes three days for the snack to come shooting out. And sometimes it takes two weeks.

You get the picture. Even if the product itself cannot be customized, your offering should always have an element of bespoke. Some ways to tailor your offering are:

- Truly understand your prospect's needs and make a creative proposal around the quantity you provide. For example, propose to charge for a certain quantity, and provide a certain additional quantity as "assessments" that will not be monetized during the initial term.

- Structure a long-term agreement with upticks as described previously.

- Link your product price to barometers of success within the client's organization. For example, if you are promoting your product as a way to cut costs, tie the price to quantifiable cost savings. If the client doesn't achieve the cost savings you promised, he pays a lower price.

- Provide non-chargeable services that complement your offering. Including essential items like training, professional support, and maintenance can go a long way in distinguishing your offering from competitors.

> **SALES HINT**
> Never accept penalty clauses in contracts. Penalty clauses encourage a confrontational relationship between buyer and seller. The only penalty clause you should ever agree to is the ultimate one—if you do not deliver what was promised, the client has the right to cancel the contract.

Many companies maintain positions on their staff for "vendor management." Frankly, this is the last person you ever want to talk to—why would you? You're not a vendor so they must not be talking about you. You are a partner who engages with the front office to understand their business needs, and then tailors an offering in line with those needs, and offers it in a creative format that incentivizes a long-term relationship.

You might ultimately have to talk to a vendor manager to conclude administrative matters like contractual documentation, but ideally you have already come to

## Secret #7: YOU ARE NOT A VENDOR

commercial terms with the business users by then. The vendor management interaction is just a formality to get the contract signed.

You are not a vendor, and don't let anyone call you one. If they do, be diplomatic about it, but tell them that you don't want to work with them as a vendor trying to sell them stuff they don't need for an inflated price. You want to engage with them as a trusted partner who is committed to a long-term meaningful relationship, and you are prepared to put your money where your mouth is to structure the contract with that in mind.

### Son's Story
### VENDOR MANAGEMENT

Careful cultivation of your contact in the "vendor management" or "procurement" departments of your client can pay huge dividends. While actual contract negotiations are often carried out with the business users of your product, procurement almost always makes an appearance near the end of the sales process to try to drive your price down further. This is literally their job, as many of them are incentivized on getting further concessions from their "vendors."

Because I don't believe that I am a vendor, it can put me at odds with the procurement people, who would like to pigeonhole me into their box of vendors.

A particularly painful example of this was when I was covering a massive multinational bank that brought my firm about US$3 million each year in revenue, and was one of our top 20 clients. I had assumed coverage on the client a couple of months prior, inheriting a wasp's nest of poorly structured contracts and uncovering usage violations on the client side that put my firm in a strong position to raise the price.

And raise the price we did, but because I was newly covering the client and hadn't put in the requisite time to build a partner-like relationship with the procurement team, my procurement contact did not take this well. In fact, he took this so poorly that after a few civilized phone conversations (him screaming at me that they weren't going to pay), he told me that they had decided to cancel my contract entirely and move all their business to my competitor.

## Secret #7: YOU ARE NOT A VENDOR

Now, while I had the full blessing of my company's management to increase the price, I did not have their blessing to lose a $3 million-per-year contract. This wasn't an acceptable outcome.

At the same time, caving on price wasn't an attractive option to me—I wanted to maintain credibility with the client by standing firm in light of their threat to cancel. Backing down now would set the tone of our relationship going forward.

I realized that the main problem wasn't so much the price as it was that we were in an adversarial relationship of vendor/client. What was the relationship I desired? As always, it was to become their trusted partner.

So faced with this pending cancellation, I had to do something that would quickly, instantaneously even, change the dynamic from vendor to partner.

One great way to do this is to link your fee structure to the client's profitability. Create a scenario where you both have some skin in the game.

I asked my procurement contact to join me in a meeting with their COO (chief operating officer). I didn't ask my contact to set up the meeting; I set up the meeting with the COO and invited my contact to join us. At that meeting I proposed a revised fee structure where we kept our price flat for the time being, but included several clauses that brought us additional revenue only if the client showed profit. Our profitability was tied to theirs.

The COO loved the proposal and eagerly agreed. The procurement guy still didn't like me too much, but he respected my commitment to come to a solution as equals, and gave up on his attempt to keep us in the hierarchical relationship of vendor/vendor management.

One year later, the client's business was booming and they ended up paying us more than they would have with my original proposal. I never heard one complaint about that though; they were content to have their fortunes linked to ours. The tied-to-profitability model was adopted as a standard approach by my company with many of our clients.

Secret #7: **YOU ARE NOT A VENDOR**

**Dad's Story**
**MY BEST STUDENT**

I have worked with a lot of wet-behind-the-ears sales people and they come in all shapes, sizes, and colors.

I was heading the advertising sales team at a television station at the time and Janice was a young woman on my staff. When I first arrived at the station, she was already there and worked as a sales assistant. As a sales assistant, her pay did not allow her the convenience of shopping at Nordstroms or Macy's, but she found some great deals at Goodwill and was careful about her appearance. She was an incredibly efficient sales assistant. She had an amazing intuition that allowed her to always anticipate what I needed and she had it ready almost before I asked.

When I took over as the general sales manager at the station, I promoted her to executive assistant. She was remarkable. Our clients loved her. Our staff loved her. Even the notoriously bad-humored news division loved her. Janice was the definition of efficiency and a joy to be around. Her smile and energy were unmatched.

One day, a couple of years after I promoted her, she came to me and said that she was ready to get into sales. My mouth dropped open and I'm pretty sure my chin hit the desk. We had never discussed anything even remotely close to that and I had no clue that she had that desire.

The words still weren't coming as I got over my shock.

Janice looked me in the eye and said, "You always told me to find people who can help me achieve my goals and then share my goals with them, right?"

True. I said this a lot. If we're going to be totally truthful about it, I probably said that a few times every day.

Janice went on. "Do you think I would be a good sales rep?"

I was still in dumb mute mode and literally could not talk. Finally I managed to squeak out something about her catching me off guard and I needed to think about it. What I was really thinking was, *What will I do without her unbelievable support?*

There was an obstacle that she wasn't aware of though. Our company had a rule that all sales, news, and programming people had to have a degree from an accredited college. Janice was the youngest of 11 children and her family did not have the resources to help her with a college education. Not wanting to assume a large debt from student loans, she chose to work instead of going to school (my guess is that she had nearly a genius IQ). I shared this dilemma with her and asked her to come up with a solution so that I could consider moving her into sales.

Fast-forward to about a month after her startling request and Janice shows up in my office and drops 25 letters of recommendation from all of my top clients onto my desk. All of the letters had one thing in common. Every letter mentioned that Janice was the only person at any station in town that they could trust 100 percent. Trust what she said, trust what she did for them, trust that she would work hard for them. And, they all formally requested that I assign her as their sales rep.

She crossed her arms and said, "Well?"

"This is impressive," I said after I had read them all. "And they are glowing. How did you get them to do it?"

"They volunteered after I told them that I wanted to get into sales."

"Janice, I can't just pass you these accounts. They are already assigned."

"I know, but I just want a chance."

## Secret #7: YOU ARE NOT A VENDOR

"I understand but I still have that other obstacle about your degree to get over."

She smiled and said, "You know my goals, so I trust that you will help me solve that one."

I called her into my office late one afternoon a couple of days later. I told her that I had received a waiver to the degree requirement if she agreed to attend a school part time with the purpose of gaining a degree. Also, the company, which had a policy of paying for graduate work for executives, would agree to reimburse her for every hour towards her degree that she completed.

"Done," she said.

Only one issue left to get through. We didn't have an open position on the sales team and I explained that she would get the first open position. She sat down in the chair in front of my desk and dropped her head for a few seconds. When she looked up she said that the clients who wrote her the letters had taken it upon themselves to contact the other stations. She then told me that she had three job offers in the last 24 hours.

"I don't want to leave," she explained, "but I really want to do sales."

Stalling for time, I asked her how she developed such loyalty from those clients when she didn't even have the authorization to make buy-and-sell decisions.

She said, "You are a good teacher and I am a good student. I listened to what you said about developing a win-win bond with the customer. I listened when you said that if the customer believes that you care more for their success than your own that they would work very hard to help you succeed. I am your best student, and soon I'm going to be your best rep."

Janice's promotion was announced the next day to the rest of the staff and they enthusiastically applauded.

Two years later she was the top producing sales rep at the station and that was from a start of absolutely nothing. Janice never did finish college, but she broke every new business record and billing record at the station.

# Secret #8

## FUTURE. POSITIVE.

*As a salesperson, you do not want to be playing therapist to your pain-stricken client. Instead, you want to have invigorating conversations about a positive future filled with desirable outcomes.*

One of the best sales books I've come across is *Let's Get Real or Let's Not Play* by Mahan Khalsa and Randy Illig. It hugely impacted how I approach client interactions and is the first book I've read that really gives a play-by-play guide to consultative selling.

The authors raise a basic premise that I believe is absolutely true, that human beings are motivated by three things: pain, gain, and novelty. We want to move away from things that hurt us (pain), move towards things that benefit us (gain), and we're willing to explore things that don't yet hurt or benefit us until we get a better idea of what they do (novelty).

Pain, gain, novelty.

This applies in the context of a sales meeting with a client; this applies to how we behave in everyday life.

This theory is often studied as behavioral psychology, which views a human being as something like an amoeba that runs away when you poke it, or moves towards sugar water if you splash a few drops near it.

Now, since human beings are not actually amoeba, we should appreciate the limitations of this model. For our context in selling though, I think it works just fine.

Look at this diagram and think about which quadrant you talk to your clients in:

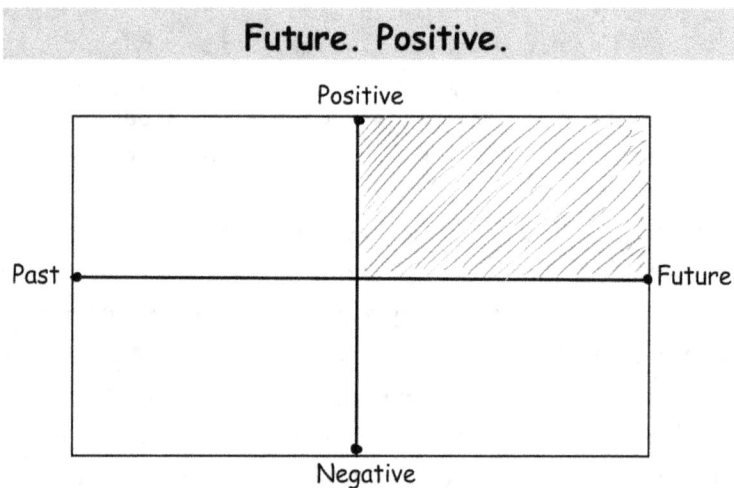

Be absolutely honest with yourself looking back on the last 10 prospect or client meetings you had and put an X in the quadrant that represents where the majority of the conversation took place for each meeting. For example, when talking to your client about a high rate of employee turnover that makes it costly for them to recruit new staff and find technical expertise, you are talking in the Past (many employees quitting)/Negative

## Secret #8: FUTURE. POSITIVE.

(and it is costly to find replacements) quadrant, with the discussion focused on pain.

You may find that many of your Xs fall into that bottom left Past/Negative quadrant. This is an easy place in which to operate. Poor salespeople will stay here forever, asking informational questions about the pain so that they aren't even selling anymore. Instead, they are providing therapy and simply commiserating with the clients about their woes. This may be valuable for the client who is delighted to have someone listen to his pain, but is it getting you any closer to the sale?

When you are trying to sell something to someone, in which quadrant do you want to be operating?

Upper right, the Future/Positive quadrant is where you want to be. Thinking back on those last 10 sales meetings, hopefully you have some Xs in the Future/Positive quadrant. How was the dynamic of the meeting different? I can guess that, at large, it was an exciting and energetic meeting filled with discussion of a positive future outcome that would benefit the client in a variety of ways.

As a salesperson, do you want to be playing therapist to your pain-stricken client? Or do you want to have invigorating conversations about a positive future filled with desirable outcomes? Future/Positive is going to get you that much closer to an actual sale.

So how does one transition from Past/Negative to Future/Positive? The key is to not ask an endless series of informational questions about Past/Negative. Find out as much as the client wants you to know, and once you have that, transition to Future/Positive.

## TURNING PAST/NEGATIVE TO FUTURE/POSITIVE

Using the previous example of high employee turnover, the conversation could look like this:

> **CLIENT**: Our employee churn is up to 27 percent annually. It's costing us way more than we have budgeted for recruiting because the headhunter fees are killing us.*
>
> **YOU**: I see, so that 27 percent churn is unacceptable in the context of your current recruiting budget and you'd like to bring the percentage down. What would be an acceptable number?
>
> **CLIENT**: We are targeting 18 percent this year, 15 percent next year.
>
> **YOU**: And by bringing it down to 18 percent or even 15 percent, what do you anticipate the positive impact on the business to be?
>
> **CLIENT**: First and foremost our employees will stay with us longer so we'll have a stronger bench of experienced and competent staff. We'll also save money on recruiting, which will enable us to move some extra budget to employee retention programs like leadership training and succession planning.

---

*Note that when talking about pain scenarios, clients will often use words that denote actual physical pain like "kill" here, or phrases like "we're bleeding."

Secret #8: **FUTURE. POSITIVE.**

**YOU**: Understood, and if you are able to maintain a deep bench of highly experienced and competent employees, what would the impact to the bottom line be?

**CLIENT**: Hmm, the first thing I can think of is that we'll become more efficient at R & D, which ultimately will make us more competitive in the market.

**YOU**: And being competitive is important to you, I take it?

**CLIENT**: Are you kidding me, it's the most important thing to us. It's how we define whether we're going to be here in 10 years.

**YOU**: I see, so we're really talking about the future sustainability of your business here.

**CLIENT**: Yes, yes we are. There is really nothing more important to us.

Let's look at each of these questions the salesperson used to quickly move out of the Past/Negative quadrant and transition to the Future/Positive one.

Right from the first question the salesperson decides not to play therapist. It would be very easy to fill meeting time with lots of informational questions like:

- Why is the turnover so high?
- What have you done already to address this issue?
- Whose fault is it?

And on and on and on. Ultimately you may end up asking these questions later, but they are not necessary for you to ask right now at a first meeting with a client who you want to speak with in the Future/Positive quadrant.

If you sense that the client wants to share more information with you, give him the opportunity to do so by asking this question: "What about the current situation is it important that I know?"

This is much more effective than asking 20 questions that are essentially targeted at finding out what about the current situation is important for you to know. Don't waste questions and valuable meeting time, just ask.

With this first question, the salesperson quickly moves from Past/Negative to Future/Positive by asking, "What would be an acceptable number?" The client has clearly thought of this and is quick to answer. What the client has not thought about in depth though is what the positive business impact is of a reduction in churn at the rate they describe. So with question two, the salesperson is acting as a partner to let the client think about the positive business result (impact to bottom line) of the desired outcome (reduction in churn to 18 percent).

The client clearly articulates the business result and the salesperson coaxes him along towards that Future/Positive with a question to allow the client to imagine the positive business result even more clearly. "If you are able to maintain a roster of highly experienced and competent employees, what would the impact to the bottom line be?"

Once you are in the Future/Positive quadrant, go ahead

## Secret #8: FUTURE. POSITIVE.

and explore it. Ask questions that encourage the client to imagine a Future/Positive scenario very clearly, like:
- What does the Future/Positive look like?
- What does it sound like?
- What does it taste like?

The stronger the image the client has of a Future/Positive, the more likely you are to get the sale. When you spend time in the Past/Negative quadrant, you merely end up with a depressed client, worn out from talking about all his issues.

With questions four and five, the salesman simply acknowledges what the client has said as a way to help him organize his thoughts. Isn't this the true job of a salesperson? To help the client organize his thoughts to imagine a Future/Positive scenario, and then provide a solution that will take the client there.

Having an understanding of the Past/Negative, Future/Positive quadrants can benefit you beyond sales. Imagine the following workplace interaction with your subordinate:

### VERSION 1 (PAST/NEGATIVE)

**SUBORDINATE**: Boss, I can't stand working with Jim. His pace is way too slow and we can't communicate.

**YOU**: That's the first I've heard of this. What sort of communication problems have you been having?

**SUBORDINATE**: Well, to start with...

## VERSION 2 (FUTURE/POSITIVE)

**SUBORDINATE**: Boss, I can't stand working with Jim, his pace is way too slow and we can't communicate.

**YOU**: I see, thanks for letting me know. What kind of pace and communication would be ideal for you?

Boom, right into Future/Positive. We've noted a problem and now let's identify a positive future. Once we've done that, it's relatively straightforward to put together some actions that will fill the gap from current pain scenario to Future/Positive.

If your client's desk is on fire, he doesn't need a salesman to come in and ask him, "How hot is the fire right now? Have you tried opening a window? Who set this desk on fire?"

What he may need is someone to ask him stimulating questions about the benefits of a Future/Positive scenario where desks never catch on fire. Stay away from Past/Negative, dwell in Future/Positive, and your clients will love to talk to you as the co-creator of their positive future.

---

*If you sense that the client wants to share more information with you, give him the opportunity to do so by asking this question: "What about the current situation is it important that I know?"*
*This is much more effective than asking 20 questions that are essentially targeted at finding out what about the current situation is important for you to know.*

Secret #8: **FUTURE. POSITIVE.**

### Son's Story
### "I HAND YOU A VIDEO..."

I use a Future/Positive technique with prospects who are not sure that what I'm selling is what they want. This technique encourages them to imagine a positive future where they've really benefitted from what I'm offering.

My new salesperson, Brenda, thought this was the cheesiest thing in the world when I first taught it to her. It may sound a little bit cheesy to you too. It's not though.

It works very well if you are engaged with the client.

Do not walk into a meeting with a new prospect and use this technique in lieu of an icebreaker. The prospect needs to be warmed up a bit first. You need him to feel comfortable with you. This technique is going to activate your prospect's imagination, and you want him to have the freedom to speak what is playing through his mind. Lack of imagination is his disease. You are the cure.

Brenda was so dubious that she demanded I show her in the next sales meeting we went to together.

"I get what you are saying," she told me, "I just don't see how it could work."

My chance came the following week. I had a casual coffee meeting set up with the head of human resources for a major bank. I had met John a couple of times in a previous role, but I hadn't developed a close relationship and we had never done business together. My goal for the meeting was for John to give me some small opening to do business together so that I could build credibility and trust by delivering beyond his expectations.

John liked meeting in coffee shops. The downside to that is the lack of privacy and it can be noisy; the upside is your prospect may be more relaxed in this casual environment, and more likely to give you information that may not be so forthcoming were you in a corporate board room.

Brenda was shadowing me for this meeting, as she had been for several weeks.

John and I had a great chat. He updated me on the current state of his business and where his focus was.

I introduced my firm and our offerings to him. He was intrigued with our offer, but far from a committed buyer.

I was able to discern that by asking him, "Having spoken now for about an hour, what ideas has this given you about where our leadership development program might be deployed in your organization?"

John nodded thoughtfully and sipped his coffee. "I'm not sure, to tell you the truth. I like what you are saying, I'm just not sure we'd see these kind of results." He was quiet again and genuinely seemed to be thinking hard. "Yes," he went on, "I just can't see how it would play out with us."

I gave Brenda a subtle nod. Here was my chance to show her that our lesson of the previous week was practical and effective.

"John, maybe I could help you crystallize your thinking on this. Can I get you to play along with me for a minute?"

"Sure, shoot."

"Say you and I meet a year from today, right here in this coffee shop."

John nodded. "Okay."

"Now during that one year, you go ahead and use our services, and some really great things happen because of them."

John nodded again. "Okay, got it."

"Now all those great scenes that play out over the year, you capture on video. When you and I meet up one

Secret #8: **FUTURE. POSITIVE.**

year from now, you hand me that video and you say, 'Brian, it's all here, all the great successes of the year.'"

John was having fun playing along. He smiled and I could almost see those positive scenes start to play out in his mind.

"Now John, you hand me that video in this coffee shop, and I say to you, 'I've got to get to another meeting in an hour. What are the two scenes on this video that you'd really like to show me right now?'"

John was completely quiet now. He wasn't nodding or moving at all; he was deep on a journey into his own mind. He was imagining these scenes I asked him to show me.

I sat in silence and let John think.

After a couple minutes he said, "Okay, I've got a few."

"Great," I told him, "Can you describe them to me?"

John went on to describe two powerful transformations in his organization that he could imagine if he used our services. This is the same person who, 10 minutes ago, was telling me that he didn't see how what I was selling could be used in his company.

John became so engaged in relating these scenes to me that the meeting went on for another 30 minutes while we explored these possibilities together.

Brenda, with a half-smile on her face, was subtly shaking her head. Either she was in awe or had pity for poor John being roped into the video technique. I'm not sure. I'll go with awe.

The meeting ended with John articulating this positive future of his imagination, and he requested that I return to his office at the same time the following week to discuss more.

We left the coffee shop and I shook John's hand. As soon as he turned to walk away, Brenda threw her arms in the air and said, "Okay, okay, it works, it works!"

# Secret #9

## ROLE-PLAY

*Just like top athletes practice intensely before a big game, masterful salespeople role-play client meetings in advance of the actual meeting. Pros know that if they are going to miss a shot, it's better to miss it in practice than in a game.*

The great thing about role-playing a client meeting (prior to the actual meeting) is that the role-play will always be harder than the actual meeting. It toughens you up for the meeting itself, and is one of the essential elements to ensuring you walk into the actual meeting extremely overprepared. Think of role-playing as intense practice before the big game.

**ROLE-PLAYS ARE STRUCTURED LIKE THIS:**

- The meeting agenda is identical to the actual client meeting.

- One or two of your office colleagues will play the prospect/client.

- You will have an audience of your peers in the

## Secret #9: ROLE-PLAY

room watching the role-play. When done, each will provide constructive comments. Start with the bad things ("the roast") and end with the good things ("the toast").

Repeat as many times as necessary until you have nailed the role-play, and you will nail the client meeting. The reason that role-plays are so hard is because you're being observed by several of your peers, and any weak points you have become not only glaringly obvious, they are discussed in great detail during the feedback session at the end of the role-play. This can be terrifying for some and simply embarrassing for others, but generally it's not a super fun time for anyone. In the beginning.

After doing a few, and by "a few" we mean literally hundreds of role-plays, you will learn to appreciate the importance, to relish the opportunity to make mistakes and then correct them in a consequence-free setting. You will come to love role-plays, and you will beg your colleagues for just one more role-play prior to your big meetings.

Pros know that if they're going to miss a shot, it's better to miss it in practice than during the game.

The tremendous upside to role-plays is that weak points will quickly be resolved when they are pointed out in glaring detail. Role-plays are a forum for dealing with a variety of objections, and you will have the benefit of the collective knowledge of your peers on how to handle those objections most effectively.

It's important that your colleagues who are playing the prospect be very well prepared as well. They need to get

> **SALES HINT**
>
> All participants in the role-play need to be committed to making it as effective as possible. Obviously you, the salesperson, should be well prepped in what you plan to deliver, your goals for the meeting, and the barometers for success. Just like you would for the actual meeting with the prospect. Put in your two hours of prep. Here are some things that you may want to think about:
>
> - What is your intent in approaching this client?
>
> - What is your desired outcome of this meeting?
>
> - What is a fallback "success factor" that, while not as good as your desired outcome, still would make the meeting outcome positive?
>
> - What are a few great questions that you can ask the client for him, not for you (e.g. to stretch his thinking and help him experience new realizations)?
>
> - What are some objections you might face and some ways that you might handle them?

into the head of that prospect, and their behavior during the role-play should mimic his. If it's known that he is the type of guy who checks his phone every three minutes during a meeting, that's exactly what should happen during the role-play. If he always shows up 10 minutes late, the person playing him should show up 10 minutes late for the role-play. Keep it as true to life as possible.

Secret #9: **ROLE-PLAY**

### Son's Story
**THE DRUNK AND BELLIGERENT ROLE-PLAY**

The hardest role-play I ever did was at an annual global sales conference. It was in a room filled with all my peers in sales from around the world, the CEO, and heads of every business line in the company. Probably 40 people all together.

My boss was announcing top performers for the year and I was in the pole position. My boss took great joy in taking the axe to his top salesmen's egos, so I knew I was in for it.

With no warning I was called up to the front of the room to perform an ad hoc role-play. I was given the scenario once I was standing in front of the room, zero time to prep, and the role-play itself was set to be two minutes long.

The scenario: You are at a Formula 1 race in Singapore in the VIP box put on by one of your clients. The business head, Sean (the guy who signs all the checks), is in the box too, and is visibly drunk. He sees you and accosts you saying, "We pay you guys way too much money, what are you trying to gouge me for today?"

No prep, in front of all my peers and senior management, and of course my boss was doing a spot on impression of a drunk and belligerent Sean.

It started out with that too much money comment, and that he couldn't believe that what I was selling was worth a million bucks.

I told him (honestly) that it was actually two million bucks they were paying us each year, and it went downhill from there…

Hardest role-play (and longest two minutes) of my life.

It wasn't an absolute catastrophe, but I definitely didn't hit it out of the park either.

But you know what, I met Sean several times after that, and while he was always a bit of a hard case, those meetings all felt like a walk in the park compared to that role-play.

# Secret #10

## STOP TRYING TO MULTITASK— YOU SUCK AT IT

*Plan your day, including what you are NOT going to do, with razor sharp focus to ensure that you free up most of your time for actual selling.*

Information overload. How many devices do you have in your life right now that make some sort of beeping noise as a call for attention? Increasingly, we are encouraged to be always on, always be available. At the beck and call of all those distracting little beeps and pop-ups.

There is nothing wrong with technology. We are absolute proponents of technological advances and effectively using technology to streamline our professional and personal lives. When the "singularity"[*] hits, we're going to be the first ones to upload our brains to hard drives. Even in a world populated by artificial intelligence and transhumans, somebody is going to have something that somebody wants. There always will be buyers and there always will be sellers, and we want to be the best sales machines in any new economy.

---

[*] Singularity is a theory that artificial intelligence is going to come to fruition within the next 50 years and will exceed human intelligence, changing human civilization radically.

That said, declining to answer every dumb mechanized beep for attention doesn't necessarily mean you are a Luddite. The master salesperson is hyper-cognizant of how many hours she has in her day, and wants to use those hours to the greatest effect possible. Greatest effect equaling the pursuit of meaningful human interactions, and then closing on sales generated through those interactions.

Technology should be used for automation. If keeping up with all of the technology you employ is a drag on your time, you've messed up somewhere. You turn the radio down to parallel park your car, what makes you think you can maintain constant vigilance on multiple information sources simultaneously?

Start focusing, stop multitasking, you suck at it!

Each day you should start with two lists. One is a high-priority list, the other is a mid-priority list. You should make these lists at the start of your day, or at the end of the day prior if you like.

> *The master salesperson is hyper-cognizant of how many hours she has in her day, and wants to use those hours to the greatest effect possible. Greatest effect equaling the pursuit of meaningful human interactions, and then closing on sales generated through those interactions.*

The most important thing for you to do on any given day is to finish the tasks on the high-priority list. That should be done to the exclusion of everything else except answering your phone. You don't want to miss out on the possibility of a meaningful human interaction.

Craft your high-priority list wisely. If it's not something that needs to be completed to the exclusion

Secret #10: **STOP TRYING TO MULTITASK, YOU SUCK AT IT**

of anything else, it shouldn't show up as a high priority.

Tailor your mid-priority list wisely as well. If it's something that is nice to do but has no urgency attached to it, put it on a separate "nice to-do" list and save it for a day when you don't have any high- or mid-priority tasks.

Clearly defining what you are *not* going to do is just as important as defining what you *are* going to do. You are not going to spend hours engaged in email dialogues that could have been handled through a three-minute phone call. You are not going to take pictures of what you ate for lunch and post them on your blog when you are back in the office. You are not going to put a high-priority task on hold simply because your boss emailed you a link to an article with the comment "great article, check this out."

Which isn't to say that you are going to ignore that article, as your boss is probably looking out for you and there might be some important information there. Forward the link over to a personal email address, and read it at your leisure later that evening in your personal time when you're relaxed and not single-mindedly focused on completing high-priority activities.

Does this sound too hard, too regimented? Does it take the fun out of your workday?

You know what's actually really fun and rewarding? Applying all of your single-minded brainpower to one task at a time, and completing that task perfectly. You know what's even more fun than that?

> *You turn the radio down to parallel park your car, what makes you think you can maintain constant vigilance on multiple information sources simultaneously?*

Making a ton of money from commissions because you are the best salesperson your firm has ever had.

You refuse to be distracted; you prioritize your day around what is going to bring the biggest buck for the bang. If you adopt these work habits, you will earn great respect from your peers and your management, you will complete your high-priority tasks in record time, and you will absolutely generate more sales.

> ### HOW RELENTLESSLY FOCUSED ARE YOU ON YOUR GOALS?
> Please play along with me for a bit.
> 
> First, think of the most challenging goal you have right now.
> 
> Please write down your answer before going on. Write it down exactly as you would answer if I asked you in person. Note any factors that might impact your answer (e.g. the "ifs" that would have to happen for this to be the case).
> 
> Here's the question:
> Are you going to achieve that goal?
> Ready to move on?
> 
> Okay, now I would like you to consider that same goal. But the scenario is a bit different this time.
> 
> Someone is holding a gun to (insert name of person you love)'s head and if you don't hit your goal by your deadline, (insert name of person you love) will take a bullet to the head.
> 
> Again, my question:
> Are you going to achieve that goal?
> This isn't realistic. It's not very pleasant either.
> 
> I don't know what your answers were but I

Secret #10: **STOP TRYING TO MULTITASK, YOU SUCK AT IT**

> can guess.
>
> So I'll leave you with this to consider. Are you as relentlessly focused on that goal as you could be?
>
> Are you going to "try" to hit that goal or will you hit that goal?

# Secret #11

## SELL IDEAS

*The holy grail of the master sales professional—selling ideas without any products and without any props.*

The most awe-inspiring salespeople are those with the ability to articulate something that can't be shown. Through that skillful articulation, they are able to make a sale.

These masterful salespeople do not rely on demos, they don't offer structured evaluations, they rarely use PowerPoint presentations. They know that the client's own imagination is much more powerful, and ultimately much more convincing, than any "prop." This is the purest form of sales and what every single one of you reading this book should aspire to in your sales career.

This is not a skill learned overnight. It is a combination of having all of the skills described up to this point learned and available to you.

Like a master craftsmen approaching his task with meticulously polished tools, the master salesperson approaches his client with his skills. He actively listens and asks powerful questions that demonstrate understanding and domain expertise. Then he listens and listens more, and when he finally does speak, he speaks of solutions that are exquisitely tailored to meet the specific needs of that client. He speaks clearly with efficacy, and by doing so demonstrates his credibility and domain expertise.

Above all, he demonstrates that he has been listening very, very closely.

This is where sales meets "visionary." Some examples of this are:

- Consultative professional services customized for each client's needs

- Entrepreneurs who sell their convictions and vision to venture capitalists

- CEOs who sell their plans for the company's future to the board

None of the above are tangible products. They cannot be demonstrated and therefore must be compellingly articulated so that the buyer can envision what he is buying without ever seeing it.

A lot of companies out there post job descriptions that say they are hiring "solution sales" or "consultative sales." In our experience, most of those companies do neither. Which isn't to say that they don't have the best intentions to do so, but selling a solution doesn't make one a solution salesperson. And rarely do these companies offer internal training programs to mold their salespeople in this way.

The consultative sale is almost always a long one (i.e.

it takes a long time to get it done). It is characterized by a deep relationship with the client. Just like men and women don't get married after a month of dating, a client is not going to buy one of these ephemeral solutions after one or two meetings.

## YOU ARE THE PRODUCT

During the long pre-sales cycle, while the foundations of the relationship are being laid, you—the sales professional—are the product. The client doesn't have a box with dials to play with, he has you in front of him listening to his problems and desires, and he needs to be absolutely convinced that you understand him. You will demonstrate that by listening, by mirroring, through tight follow-ups that are on target with what was discussed.

You will be patient, some of these sales could take more than a year to conclude. You will always progress the discussion forward, small relevant follow-ups that over time mean big progress. You will not sell your client an overpriced banana today; you will give him the banana for free and sell him the whole banana plantation 12 months from now.

> *The consultative sale is almost always a long one (i.e. it takes a long time to get it done). It is characterized by a deep relationship with the client. Just like men and women don't get married after a month of dating, a client is not going to buy one of these ephemeral solutions after one or two meetings.*

Secret #11: **SELL IDEAS**

The salesperson doesn't decide the timing of the sale, the client does. There may be external factors, the economy for example, that will delay or progress a sale. The master salesperson understands that and is consistent in his or her approach.

Imagine that you are absolutely taken with a beautiful girl, but that girl has turned you down for a date. Imagine if you asked her out on a date every month for the next 12 months. You try different ways, but for the first 12 months she always has an excuse for saying no. Come month 13 you ask her out and she says, "Yes, I'd love to go to dinner with you."

What changed?

Your approach could have something to do with it. What changed most though were her feelings about you. Some months when you asked her out, she had a boyfriend or had just broken up with a boyfriend. Other months, she was out of town or had taken up a new hobby and was busy on the weekends.

Month 13 though, she didn't have a boyfriend, she was in town, and she was feeling a little bit lonely because she had watched a sad movie the night before. And there you were with a well-timed, nonaggressive, and tailored offer ("I know you love Indian food. I read an article about a new place that just opened, I'd love to try it with you."). And this time she said *yes*.

---

### PERSISTENCE

A high school boy had heard rumors that his next-door neighbor, a Japanese man, was a master of Japanese sword fighting. The boy wanted nothing more in the world than to learn a martial art, so he knocked on his neighbor's door and when the Japanese wife answered, he said, "I heard that your husband is an expert in the Japanese sword and I was hoping that he could give me lessons."

The woman smiled and called her husband who came to the door with a stern expression and said to the boy in his heavily accented English, "No fighting sword here, go home." He brusquely waved the boy off, slamming the door in his face.

Not deterred (this kid was obsessed with samurai movies and couldn't think of anything cooler than learning how to use a Japanese sword), the boy went back to the house the next day. Again the wife answered the door, the husband was called, and they repeated nearly an identical discussion as the day prior.

The boy went back to the door every day for the next 365 days and asked the same question, and every day got the same answer. It became a bit of a game, sometimes the wife would serve him green tea or give him a cookie, and then the husband would arrive and shoo him away.

On day 366, the boy went to the door as usual. Unusually, it was the husband who answered.

The boy asked his question, "I understand that you are a master of the samurai sword, and it would be a great privilege if you could instruct me."

The husband bowed deeply and formally to the boy and said, "I have been waiting for you. Your lessons begin today."

The boy started his swordsmanship training immediately, and became a world-renowned expert in Japanese martial arts.

## Secret #11: SELL IDEAS

There is no place for giving up in the master salesman's repertoire. Your client's moods may be capricious, but yours never are, because you have the strength of your convictions. Like a marathon runner, you are committed to finishing the race at a steady pace.

Your conviction is hard earned. You employ each of the principles described here as appropriate. If what you can offer does not match the client's needs, you acknowledge that—to both the client and yourself.

You can earn great credibility by saying, "Based on what I've learned from discussing this with you, I don't think I have anything that will meet your needs right now. I hope you can give me some time to consider this, and approach you again once that has changed."

You regroup and spend as much time as you need to come up with something more suitable.

Keep in mind that until you have the right offer, it is you who are the product. Leaving the client alone for eight months and then picking up the phone and calling him one day to re-engage is not the right approach.

While you are creating an offer, no matter how long it takes, be thoughtful about that client, be committed to strengthening the relationship. Meet him for drinks and send him relevant articles when you come across them. Use these small touch points to maintain and grow your human interactions.

> *If what you can offer does not match the client's needs, you acknowledge that—to both the client and yourself.*

You will find that there is nothing more satisfying than concluding a sale that took many months or years.

*Stop Sucking At Sales*

A sale that might have never happened if not for your commitment to go knocking on the door every single day like that high school boy who wanted to learn the sword.

Secret #11: **SELL IDEAS**

### Son's Story
### BUILDING TRUST

The company I worked for was in the business of providing highly specific analysis to investment banks. The product was tailored for each bank based on that bank's model and there was no similar service or product in the market. We also had strong media relationships, and our analyses frequently showed up in articles in financial media like *The Wall Street Journal* (*WSJ*) and *Financial Times*. It wasn't cheap. We worked on a subscription model, and our analyses, which helped banks position themselves competitively versus their banking peers in the market, sold for around US$1 million per year.

One day, our analysis appeared in an article on the front page of *Nikkei Shimbun*, the premier financial newspaper in Japan, akin to the *WSJ* in the United States. The article was incendiary in that it used our data to rank Japanese investment banks on the success of their core business, and some of them weren't looking so good.

The day that it appeared we got a call from one of the top three banks in Japan (well, everybody thought they were one of the top three until that article appeared and showed they weren't even one of the top five).

The person who called was irate, screaming over the phone that our data was wrong, wanting to know how we could do this, and telling us we had insulted him and the bank. He demanded an immediate retraction and apology.

This gentleman was Mr. Okumoto, the head of strategy for the bank, extremely senior in the organization. After I let him run through the invective and burn himself out a little bit, I offered to come by and explain what the underlying information was that made up that report. He accepted, clearly welcoming the chance to berate me in person.

The meeting wasn't extremely pleasant, but it was successful in the sense that he spent two hours telling me why we were wrong—in essence two hours telling me all about his business.

My team and I walked out of that room with a fantastic understanding of that bank's processes, their worldview, their aspirations, and how they benchmarked themselves against their peers. I had been trying to get a meeting like this with that bank for more than a year.

The follow-up to the meeting was that we sent Mr. Okumoto some detailed analysis to clarify where our report came from. He couldn't argue with the data, which was entirely accurate, but he did have some questions and, again, I went in to visit him and spent considerable time making sure that it was absolutely clear. I essentially armed him with the information that he needed to present to senior management.

None of this was selling, but all of it was relationship building. I had no obligation to spend that kind of time ensuring that he understood data from a product that he didn't even pay for. Yet I approached it as if he were the most valuable paying client we had.

From then on, I orchestrated my internal team to approach our meetings with him like a sales engagement. He would ask for clarification on something and we would provide that, along with some new information we knew would be relevant to him based on our increased understanding of his business.

This first time that the relationship finally changed from combative to curious was after about 12 months. He was getting such value from the additional analyses we were providing that he started to show interest in the product itself, even asking if he could see it live.

At that point we switched gears from defending our position to pitching our offering. Japanese clients are especially thoughtful when considering large-scale implementations of this nature, and once we had convinced Mr. Okumoto, we still had to spend another 12 months building consensus among other decision makers within the bank, finally concluding the sale after two years.

For all of us involved in that long process, this was tremendously satisfying. There were moments of doubt along the way, but we also had the strength of our convictions:

- The client clearly had a need, although he hadn't yet identified that latent need openly to us.

- We had great confidence in the strength of our offering and, as we understood Okumoto's business increasingly well, knew that it fit his latent need.

- We approached every engagement as if Mr. Okumoto was our most valued client, demonstrating the level of service he could expect should he ever become a paying client.

- In spite of small frustrations and setbacks (halfway through the process Mr. Okumoto moved to a different division and we had to build the relationship from zero with his replacement), we maintained the strength of our convictions, never oversold, and remained committed to the integrity of our offering and our high asking price.

Once the sale was complete, we knew the client so well that it was almost like we were their employees. They saw us as true partners, and the implementation went smoothly and, as expected, brought great value to their business.

Secret #11: **SELL IDEAS**

### Dad's Story
### HOME AND GARDEN TELEVISION (HGTV)

In the spring of 1994, I got a call from a friend of mine in the radio business. I was running a television station in Reno, Nevada, at the time. My good friend Ed asked what I was doing and whether I was happy.

My answer, always the same, was that I was doing great and was very happy.

Ed's response was typical to our relationship and he told me, "You can't BS a BSer." And then he proceeded to tell me about his friend and former colleague from Scripps Networks, Ken, who had recently been relieved of his duties as the head of the Scripps radio division because they had sold all of the stations. He said that Ken had decided to pursue a dream that he had been shaping for the past few years to launch a cable network based around the "home and garden."

I listened, but didn't quite get it.

"Anyway," Ed said, "Ken asked me to head up the sales department and I had to turn him down because I am doing my own start-up radio group."

He said that he had recommended me for the position.

I told Ed that I was flattered but knew nothing about sales at a cable network. He said that was okay because neither did Ken or anybody connected to the project.

I said that was encouraging and that it was perfectly set up for failure.

"Who would invest in something like that?"

He said that Scripps had already committed US$25 million to the venture.

"Let me get this straight," I said, "The company that

just fired Ken is now going to fund his cable network?"

"Yep."

"How many cable networks had Scripps launched before this one?" I asked.

"None!"

Another good sign.

A few days later Ken called me himself. And truth be told, I was not particularly enjoying my current job for various reasons even though the station was experiencing unprecedented success. Ken and I talked for an extended period of time and he convinced me to take a trip to Knoxville, Tennessee, the new location of the Home and Garden Network.

A couple of weeks later, I flew to Knoxville, where I got to experience the awesome energy of a small group of people already committed to joining this new start-up. None, by the way, with much cable network experience.

There was a lady from Detroit who was recruited to lead the affiliate team; she had been in the cable industry for a few years. Ken had recruited a programming specialist who was currently teaching at Syracuse University and had experience at CBS, one of the top US TV networks. His assistant came from the news department at the CBS TV station in Los Angeles, California. Between the two of them, they had never programmed a single day of content for any network. But they were brilliant and tireless. The new head of operations had never built an infrastructure to sustain the enormous load a cable network required.

In the end, he not only built the network infrastructure but also all of the facilities that would later win awards and become emulated by many, many networks.

I accepted the position at less of a compensation package than I would have liked, but the challenge was so alluring that I just had to be a part of it. I moved to Knoxville,

Tennessee, ahead of my family. This turned out to be a good thing because the workload was beyond comprehension and I had no time to myself. I worked along with everybody at the network 18 to 20 hours a day, seven days a week. Ken rarely went home before 3 a.m. and was back in the office by 9 a.m. the next day.

Our goal was to launch by October of the same year, something that had never been done before. Normal time to launch was more than twice the time we were reaching for. Our budget was tight so we carefully watched everything we spent. The cost of producing content for the network was very expensive, as were the marketing and promotions we needed to get the word out.

It's easy to look at the success of HGTV now and say that it was a no-brainer; but let me say that nobody at that time could have predicted that it would be this successful. It was a very difficult sell for people to give up their good jobs and come and join a new network that was about paint drying and grass growing. One of my potential clients actually said that to me and walked out of the room laughing. We didn't have the budget to pay the going rate for good salespeople. Far from it, we paid less than half the going rate for a cable network salesperson.

Did it cause me concern? Absolutely.

Did I lose sleep? I don't remember having a good night's sleep for over six months.

I would wake up in the middle of the night in a hotel room and have moments of panic wondering where I was. In St. Louis, Ken and I finished a meeting with the Ralsten Purina CEO and his marketing team at 3 a.m. at Morton's Steak House. We caught our next flight at 6 a.m. for a meeting we had scheduled with Pier One at 9 a.m., and then followed up with two ad agencies and one more client before catching a flight to Los Angeles to meet with more potential clients. All in all, we traveled to nine cities in seven days and conducted over 25 presentations. In between, I was trying to hire sales staff.

The following is the hiring strategy that I settled on after being turned down by several people already involved in cable network sales:

1. Look for bright, young people with little or no experience in network cable sales.

2. Seek out people from a similar industry that may not pay as well as cable sales.

3. Seek advice from agency media supervisors about people they would recommend. This also got the attention of agency decision makers about our network without the pressure of selling them anything.

4. Stop recruiting; get the word out that we are looking for highly motivated people and that cable network sales experience was not required.

The result was mixed as far as quality, but we had a lot of interest. We got calls from salespeople at TV rep firms, major magazines, and local television stations. I set up telephone interviews with all respondents to tell them about the new network concept, what the position required and what the pay range was. I then said that I would be in such and such a place for interviews. If they were interested they could follow up with my assistant (I did manage to hire one of those after three months) to set the time. Then I waited to see if they would ask any questions.

Most asked basic questions such as how soon would we be ready to hire (immediately); was there any room in the salary range (no); where is the office in New York (don't know yet); how many salespeople are you going to hire (one, maybe two). Okay then, call Helen if you want to interview.

They weren't great questions. These generally weren't mature, polished salespeople. And I was okay with that; I would work with them. Then I got a call from a sales manager at *Time* magazine. Her name was Laurie and what follows is the first telephone conversation I had with Laurie as close as I can remember it:

"Steve, it is Steve right? Would you like to save a little time?"

"What do you mean?"

"Well, do you mind if I ask you some pointed questions?"

"Not at all, go ahead."

"Are you trying to fill some space in your office or are you really interested in getting a kick-ass salesperson?"

"Good question," I said, "I want a super star not yet discovered. I want a 'rainmaker.'"

"The home and garden industry is very lucrative for the magazine media. Are you aware of that?"

"Yes, and I have talked to some reps from that group."

"Were you impressed?"

"Slightly," I said.

"You shouldn't be, because everyone I know in magazine sales is an order taker."

"I said 'slightly,' not 'very.'"

"Ha, okay, just so you know that I am not an order taker."

"And you also don't sell in the home and garden category if you work for *Time*."

"I know, but what do you think is harder to sell: gardening or bad news? My team leads the sales for *Time* magazine."

"Why do you want to switch?" I asked.

"Didn't say I did, but if I did it would be for a position that fit my skill set and had a very, very high upside."

"I don't know what the upside is and I will not oversell the position."

She got more assertive. "What is your experience in network sales? Are you hiring a consultant in New York to get you agency introductions? Have you made any agency presentations there yet? If so, what was the response?"

"None. Maybe. No." I was sounding meek now.

"Well, save your money on the consultant and let's get going."

"What?"

"Steve, you have already missed the upfront selling season and the only money left is what's known as scatter. Do you know what that is?"

"Not really."

"What is your budget for the year?"

"I told you that I don't have a lot of money to spend."

"No, I mean what is the number you have to hit for sales next year?"

"Between $2 and $4 million. Not exactly set yet."

"Good, tell them you'll do the $4 million, but you'll need a little more money to pay the salespeople. Can you do that?"

"What makes you so certain?"

"Because I am that good," she said. "I've got to get on another call. When shall we meet up?"

"What's good for you?"

"I have a boot camp workout tomorrow but I can meet you after at 7:30?"

"A.m. or p.m.?"

"A.m. of course."

I gave her the address of my hotel and hung up.

## Secret #11: SELL IDEAS

I turned to my assistant, Helen, and said that I just talked to my new head of our New York office. I said that this woman had just thrown the line in the water and hooked me like a big bass.

We met about two weeks later and Laurie presented one of the most thought-out strategic proposals I had ever seen. I didn't hire her on the spot, although I was tempted. I wanted to see what her follow-up would be like. That night she called me at my hotel (no mobile phones yet) and asked how my day had gone. I told her she ruined it for the rest of the interviewees.

"When can you start?" I asked.

"We'll see," she said, laughing. "Get a good night's sleep and we can start negotiating tomorrow." It took two weeks to negotiate a deal that she was going to be happy with, and for the next five years, Laurie and her team exceeded their sales goals, stretch goals, and super stretch goals every single year.

Laurie was truly a warrior and never, ever slowed down. She was maybe 5'3", 105 pounds, and had the drive and heart of a professional athlete. She ended up making more money than anyone at the network except for Ken by her third year.

Have you noticed that good salespeople are suckers for good salespeople? We love being sold by a good seller. Laurie was a great seller, and I knew it that first day I spoke to her on the phone.

She didn't have a product to show me or proof of what she was offering, but she had amazing talent for building castles out of sand, and an even greater talent for getting her prospects to see the castles as well.

# Secret #12

## CELEBRATE WINS, FORGET DEFEATS

*In sales, as in sports, sometimes you win and sometimes you lose. Great competitors know how important it is to minimize the setbacks while celebrating the victories.*

In sales, as in sports, sometimes you win and sometimes you lose.

Losing a sale can be a soul-destroying experience. You have committed a huge amount of your time and your company's resources. You were engaged with the client through multiple meaningful human interactions and you accurately identified their needs and tailored a proposal that you truly believe met those needs. You structured your commercials creatively and indicated your willingness to be flexible.

But you still lost the sale.

Macroeconomic factors or your client's internal politics might have influenced the decision, or your competitor might simply have had a better product or proposal than you.

**YOU'VE DONE EVERYTHING RIGHT. YOU:**

- Know how the prospect wants to be sold

### Secret #12: CELEBRATE WINS, FORGET DEFEATS

- Know what his real needs are
- Know that your solution is right
- Know that he is the decision maker
- Have a solid relationship
- Addressed all the objections and turned them into positive aspects of your solution

But, they didn't move forward with the sale. Why?

You may begin to question the techniques. Don't. In every sale opportunity there are hidden agendas that you will never bring to the surface. Understand that and move on, right?

Well, not quite. It is important to always salvage something from the experience.

## HERE'S WHAT YOU DO:

1. **Respond to the decision not to move forward with a positive affirmation.**
   "Susan, I understand that this may be the wrong time to buy, but do you mind sharing with me the reason for the delay? I'd like to share your concerns with my management so that we can better anticipate your needs."

   You are not giving up on the sale so you use the term "delay."

2. **Get a confirmation for your solution.**
   "Susan, do you still think that what I have proposed

will (solve/enhance/produce) the results we discussed?"

3. **If the answer is "not sure," you need to gently probe. You might say, "Good, I want you to be 99 percent sure that we can solve your problem. Can you be specific as to *any* of your concerns?"**
   Understand that the client may not want to share "hidden agendas" because it may be too personal or embarrassing. Do not try to close again. Suggest a follow-up meeting down the road. Sixty days at the earliest. Give the hidden issues time to resolve themselves.

4. **Ask for a referral.**
   "If you think I can help out anyone you might know who needs a similar solution would you mind telling them about me?"

   This is when you will know if they really appreciate you because they will immediately give you names of people they know. Never ask the prospect to call on your behalf but always ask if you can use their name when you call. If you get an appointment through one of their referrals you should call to let them know and thank them for their help.

You will get their business eventually. You have invested time, energy, and thought into your prospect and you will win. Nothing that you sincerely pursue will go unrewarded.

What do you do when you lose? Like an athlete, a loss will drive you to practice harder. It's not hard work that always wins though, it's smart work. The first thing you need to do after a loss is wash that loss off. The next thing you do, and do this quickly, is a post-mortem loss review with your team.

## THE DAY OF

The day you lose the sale is not a good day to talk about it. In fact, you're done for the day. Go home, hit a punching bag, or go to your local pub. Do whatever you need to get that loss out of your system. The rule is that you can moan about it as much as you want the day it happens, but self-pity is over when you wake up the next day.

## THE DAY AFTER

Wake up, brush the loss off, put on your best suit and spend a long time making sure your tie knot or hair is perfect. Loss, what loss? The loss is stuck in that cool little dream catcher you have mounted above your bed.

Go to work and schedule a debriefing meeting for that day, inviting everyone who had a key role in the sales engagement.

1. When scheduling the meeting, ask each person to

come to the meeting with three mistakes that were made during the engagement.

2. During the meeting, go quickly through the room and allow each person to voice their three comments. This process will uncover any overlap.

3. Record these points in *The Book of Mistakes We Will Never Make Again*.

This loss review meeting isn't particularly fun for anyone. It requires you to take an unflinching view of where you went wrong. But how are you going to avoid the same pitfalls in the future if you aren't crystal clear on what those pitfalls are?

Once the loss review is done, the loss is done. You've wallowed in the mud long enough; it's time to get on with it. In fact, you are now going to schedule another meeting with the exact same group of people for the following day.

And the topic of that meeting is: How you are going to win the lost business back.

Did your potential client sign a two-year exclusive deal with your competitor? Then now is the time to craft your two-year vision, strategy, and action timeline that is going to result in the client switching to you in exactly two years from now.

---

*Loss, what loss? The loss is stuck in that cool little dream catcher you have mounted above your bed.*

---

Secret #12: **CELEBRATE WINS, FORGET DEFEATS**

## WINNING

Let's now address the more pleasant topic of winning.

Nothing is more satisfying than closing a deal. This is why you became a salesperson. You get a physical rush when that signed contract comes back and you hold it in your hand for the first time. We (father and son) have been doing this for a combined 55 years, and we still get that rush.

Losses should be quickly reviewed and forgotten. Wins should be drawn out, celebrated, and glorified. Your best wins should be recorded in company lore and told around the campfire for years to come and passed on to future generations. The whole office should know. You should have a win song that you blast on your computer speakers while you perform a choreographed win dance at your desk. Win dance should include the moonwalk, the worm, and lots of high fives. The other salespeople should know of your victory, they should dance with you. Their jealousy at your impressive sale will drive them harder to achieve their own wins.

Wins generate momentum. They create big waves that you can surf to more wins. Wins motivate you, your sales colleagues, and all the internal resources who were so integral to your win.

## REDISTRIBUTE PRAISE

As a salesperson, you are rewarded by the win, the praise it brings, and the commissions. What's the first thing that every single salesperson in the world does when he wins a deal? He does some quick math in his head or on a calculator and figures out how much money he just put in his pocket.

You are motivated by commissions; it's one reason why you became a salesperson. This is not an ugly thing. It's a beautiful thing. Elegant in its black and white simplicity. Win or lose.

There is something that is absolutely essential to keep in mind though. Very rarely are you the sole architect of this success. You were supported internally in multiple ways by many colleagues—your sales administrator, your legal department, your product specialists...the list goes on.

These people do not get commissions. That's fine. If they want commissions they should consider a career in sales. But, it is absolutely essential, and it is your responsibility, to ensure that they are praised for their contribution.

> You are motivated by commissions; it's one reason why you became a salesperson. This is not an ugly thing. It's a beautiful thing. Elegant in its black and white simplicity. Win or lose.

Here are some things you can do to show appreciation to those involved in the successful sale:

1. Write a personal email to each person integral to the successful sale, copying each of their bosses.

2. Write a note directly to his or her boss, describing what value that person brought to the process.

## Secret #12: CELEBRATE WINS, FORGET DEFEATS

3. Write a similar note to the CEO.

4. Schedule a team outing—drinks or dinner. You are paying, and don't be stingy on the fine wines.

I have a pretty simple rule—if I'm out with colleagues at a bar (colleagues who have or will contribute to my success), drinks are on me. That might cost me a few hundred dollars a few times a year, but in the long term, investing a few hundred dollars in showing your appreciation is insignificant in relation to how much business these colleagues help you to win.

It's not just a matter of putting your credit card behind the bar. Take the time to order their drinks or food. Hand them their drinks and clink glasses in toast and tell them how much you appreciate them.

Most people in any organization are starving for praise. A little thanks can go a long way in earning loyalty and the respect of your peers.

### Dad's Story
### THE COMEBACK

I was selling television advertising in Portland, Oregon, and had only been with the station one month when the local sales manager gave me a referral. The company was a furniture chain, but it did not have a store in our market. They had requested a proposal from our station and it was clear that the other four stations in the market got the same RFP (request for proposal). The proposal was due the following day.

I immediately got on the phone and called the contact given on the RFP and got a "He's not available to take your call" message from the gatekeeper.

I said that he was expecting my call. She put me through and I told him that I received the RFP for my station and I needed to ask some very quick questions so I could give him exactly what he needed.

Thirty minutes later I had found out that they were opening a store in Portland in 90 days and wanted to prime the pump. He wanted to advertise on shows that gave him the biggest reach and the most impact for his dollar. The RFP didn't give an ad budget, but it did say that they would make their decision on the most viewers reached for the lowest price. I set up a time to meet him face-to-face.

I spent several hours researching furniture stores and finding just the right programs to reach his goals. We met and went over the proposal in detail. I was the only sales rep who made the trip to meet him in person. I toured his store, bought him lunch, and talked about his vision for his company.

We hit it off.

## Secret #12: CELEBRATE WINS, FORGET DEFEATS

I presented the proposal and explained every decision I had made for him. He said he liked it and that it made perfect sense. I asked if the television commercial had already been produced and he said it had. I requested a copy to take back with me. He agreed. I was sure I had won a very lucrative deal.

Two days later he called and asked me to make a copy of the commercial and take it to my competitor. I asked if he was splitting the buy and he said no, he was giving the whole thing to one of my competitors and I was not on it at all.

Talk about the wind taken out of your sails!

I didn't know what to say and hung up. I made a copy of the ad and took it to the other station. I called back the next day to tell him that I had taken care of the delivery and then I asked him why he had changed his mind.

He told me, "I never said you had the buy. I said I like what you presented but the other stations gave me prime time* shows at the same price you were selling your earlier time slots. You didn't include any prime time on your proposal."

I didn't argue because I had already explained to him that summer prime time viewing was a waste of dollars because all the shows were repeats up to three times over. So, I had presented only shows that were new including late night viewing because they got the highest ratings.

I just thanked him for being honest and asked if I could stay in touch.

Every week I sent him a copy of the ratings for prime time viewing and it proved my point. I called him after his campaign had run for about six weeks and said I hoped that

---

*Prime time TV are the hours between 8-11 p.m. that get the most viewers and therefore command the highest ad price.

everything was going well and that he was happy with the results.

He asked when I could come and see him again, and I asked him for what.

They had done market research and that less than one percent of the sample remembered anything about his company from the commercials.

I stayed silent.

And then he asked me, "What do you think I should do?"

I reminded him of the reason I left prime time off my proposal and that he should buy my competitor's non-prime programming.

He said there was no way was he going to do that because I was the only rep who had stayed in touch with him and given him good answers. He had already cancelled the other stations that morning and wanted to see what I could do.

"I'll be in your office tomorrow, but my original proposal still stands."

The next day he bought me lunch and put the entire buy on my station. The campaign was successful and he opened his store a month later to great business. A few months later I was promoted to general sales manager, but I never passed that client to any of my guys because he wouldn't work with anyone else. He tried to hire me a half dozen times and I told him that he didn't need to pay me to work for him because I did it for free anyway.

He couldn't argue with that.

Secret #12: **CELEBRATE WINS, FORGET DEFEATS**

**Son's Story
BURN THE BOATS**

Remember that huge deal I won with the Japanese bank (Secret #11: Sell Ideas)?

Well, they cancelled.

As much as it pains me to recall that loss, here's the sad story.

I sold the bank my product on a three-year contract. Each year the price upticked significantly until year three, when they would be paying full price. For the first three years, while the price upticked, the client was locked in and could not cancel. After year three, we had a contractual clause that allowed us to increase the price each year in line with inflation. So due to inflation, the client would end up paying around a three percent increase each year. This was a clever clause we enacted to ensure our margins were not eroded through inflation, and I'm surprised that more companies don't take this precaution.

Three percent doesn't sound like much, but you take notice when it's three percent of a million bucks.

My client's usage of the product had slipped, and my key contact had been transferred to a different department, so I didn't feel we were ideally embedded when year four and the inflationary increase came around.

In situations like this, I liked to hold off on sending over the invoice with a price increase until I had met and spoken with the client. In some cases, I waived the increase if I thought there was a danger it could lead to a cancellation.

What I had found was that—with some companies—as long as the invoice amount was the same each year, they just kept paying; but if that number changed at all, up or down even one dollar, it sent off a red flag and I would start getting calls from financial controllers wondering why the invoice amount had changed.

I made a call to our finance department.

"Hey, Tim, this is Brian in Hong Kong. Do me a favor and hold off sending any uptick invoices to M Bank."

"Hold. Off. Invoices. For. M Bank," Tim repeated, clearly writing it down on a Post-it or something.

"Did you write that down on a Post-it or something, because this is a big deal and I am going to have issues if you send anything."

"Not a problem, mate." (Tim was in our UK office.) "I'll put a note in the system."

"Thanks, Tim. I'll let you know when we're good to go."

I put the phone down, reassured, and got back to what I was doing.

A week later I get a call from my client contact. She wanted to ask me some details of the price increase on the invoice she had just received.

I called Tim.

"Tim, did you send an invoice to that Japanese bank after all?"

"What bank was that, mate?"

Trying to teach a pig to sing was not on my list of to-do items for that day.

I flew to Japan and meticulously explained the contractual price increase to my client. They were extremely polite and understanding. I flew back to my home base in Hong Kong and three days later they called to cancel the contract.

I don't take losses well, but I do follow my own advice. I didn't tell anyone about the cancellation. I hung up the phone and, although it was 4 p.m. on a Tuesday, walked out of the office and straight to a bar. Five double martinis

## Secret #12: CELEBRATE WINS, FORGET DEFEATS

later I was close to forgetting my name, not to mention the cancel.

I gathered the stakeholders the following morning and told them what happened. I recalled that my meeting invitation read something like "M Bank Post-Mortem," so some of them probably got the hint when they read that.

It was an uncomfortable meeting for all of us, but perhaps most uncomfortable for me thanks to my hangover.

We went around the room, each of us coming up with one thing we could have done better, and one idea for winning the business back. We wrote it all down and then we adjourned and life went on.

Well, it wasn't actually as pain-free as that. The CEO and entire management team were calling me all day to find out what happened.

I developed PTSD (Post Traumatic Stress Disorder) and flinched like a cowed dog every time my phone rang.

Things died down after about a week. I do recall getting an email from our managing director that said something like, "Do whatever it takes to win this back. Burn the boats." Ugh.

There was no way that my contacts in Japan were buyers in the short term. It was a global bank though, and other regions hadn't been exposed to the product. If it worked for them in Japan, I thought it might work for them anywhere.

I got busy with my Rolodex and after a half-day of calling in favors, ended up with the email and phone number of the COO for the same bank in New York.

I then invested the next six months in making a case for the bank to use my product in their New York office, ultimately winning the business, although at a significantly reduced price compared to the contract that was cancelled. It was somewhat of a happy outcome, but I would rather have not lost the business in the first place.

# Secret #13

## KEEP A DIARY

*You don't remember what you had for lunch on Monday, so how could you possibly remember what you discussed with a client three months ago?*

One of the key behaviors that define master salespeople is rigorously recording all client interactions, and being hyper-communicative within the organization about who was met and what was discussed.

Any serious company will have some sort of CRM system. We have used many in our careers—SAP, Salesforce, Siebel, and proprietary in-house systems to name a few.

The system doesn't matter. What matters is the content. How good the content is depends entirely on you.

The best salespeople are hyper-communicative. They broadcast their strategies for their clients company-wide. They prep for client meetings as a team, and they return from meetings to share what they have learned with the same team. Keeping a written record of all client engagements is essential to this process. Not only are you doing a brain dump for yourself, you are also keeping a record for posterity. Client coverage gets changed around sometimes. Wouldn't you like to start covering a new client with the benefit of a written record of every single meaningful human interaction someone from your company had with that client for the last five years?

If your company doesn't have a CRM in place, you should start petitioning for them to get one. Or for the more Machiavellian of you, don't bother. Just develop your own way of tracking meetings and enjoy what it feels like to be top sales dog year after year.

You don't need to be writing prize-winning short stories for each recap, but you should capture all the relevant information to a fair level of detail.

1. When did the interaction occur?
2. Where did the interaction occur?
3. Who did you meet?
4. What was the topic for the meeting and the agenda?
5. What was discussed?
6. What are the follow-ups, and who from your firm is the owner of that follow-up?
7. Other seemingly inconsequential information: What kind of music your client likes? Did he just get back from a week in Thailand? Does he run triathlons in his spare time? Did he take his coffee black or with cream?

This is very much a case of junk in, junk out. Stick to the relevant points and the key action items that arose from the meeting.

"But how my client takes his coffee is irrelevant," you point out.

To that, we reply that a prerequisite to building trust with your client is to know your client. When Ross visits you at your office and you nonchalantly give him a coffee just the way he likes it, believe me, he'll notice.

The next time you go in to visit the client, review your recap prior. You'll be surprised at how much you've already forgotten and at how helpful this will be in planning for the next meeting.

Secret #13: **KEEP A DIARY**

### Son's Story
**THE TRAVELING SALESMAN'S APPROACH TO CRM**

IBM is a strong sales organization with rigorous sales training and processes. They are relentless in tracking client interactions.

As told to me by an ex-IBMer, he was required to submit full write-ups of every client meeting within 24 hours of the meeting. The problem was that this salesman covered the Midwest of the United States from his home office, and his days were filled with driving by car from meeting to meeting across the three or four states that he covered. It was physically impossible for him to get the write-ups done in the prescribed time, and he was frequently penalized through deductions from his commissions for failing to comply.

This salesman was a clever guy. He graduated from a top university, and then went to Europe where he completed his MBA. He decided to apply some thought to this dilemma and came up with a brilliant solution. He started dictating his meeting recaps into a recorder while he was driving between meetings. At the end of the day he then emailed the full recording to a third party who transcribed the entire file into writing and sent it back to him by email.

He never missed the 24-hour deadline again. His boss didn't know what had changed; he was just happy that he was obeying the rules. It cost my acquaintance a bit out-of-pocket to have the transcription done, but it was significantly less than the commissions he had been losing through penalties. He also found great value in those comprehensive recaps, which were much more detailed than he had been submitting before, and effectively used his increasingly rich client database to grow the revenue from his territory.

# Secret #14

## THE PERFECT WEEK

*Learn some techniques to suspend your limiting belief system and dramatically improve your performance in sales and in life.*

We're going to get a little weird here; bear with us. Some people exhibit talents that appear to transcend the norm whether in sports, music, languages, business, and yes, in sales. How do they do that? Some work harder. Some work smarter. Some do both.

But the really amazing ones do something different. They harness the power of their minds in ways that you may have never considered. This is akin to the "zone" that great athletes sometimes refer to. Everything moves in slow motion, very clearly, as the athlete effortlessly outperforms his competition.

"Flow" is the mental and physical state in which a person performing an activity is fully immersed in a feeling of energized focus, full involvement, and enjoyment in the process of the activity. In essence, flow is characterized by complete absorption in what one does. The ego has fallen to the wayside and nothing hinders this amazing feeling of connectedness.

My dad has been fascinated with the mysteries of the

mind from an early age when he saw a television show where Stanford researchers hypnotized a guy and told him to put his whole arm in a pot of cold water for two minutes. Which he did. Except the water was boiling. And when he took his arm out there were no signs of burns or any damage, and his skin temperature was eerily normal. (Don't try this at home.)

Wanting more, he read voraciously on the subject, including a book by Dr. Maxwell Maltz called *Psycho Cybernetics*. Cybernetics referred to a fairly new (in the 1960s) science of computer programming. Maxwell mashed this up with psychology, suggesting that people could program their life the way they would like to live it, including the outcomes. Maltz was the forerunner of self-help gurus like Zig Ziglar and Tony Robbins. The "programming" process included discipline, imagination, vision, belief, and emotion.

> The subconscious mind can be likened to a genius three-year-old... It has incredible processing power, but likes to be spoken to in simple, single-syllable words, which paint vivid images and inspire deep emotions.
>
> **—Gerald Kein, hypnotherapist**

My dad continued his research into the power of the mind and its practical applications. He took a seminar that taught the participants to walk barefoot across burning coal without getting burned. He took a course from a Native American and at the end of the three-day seminar, took the sharp point of a wooden arrow, put it against the soft portion of his neck just below his Adam's apple, put the feathered end against the wall and pushed with his entire body (no hands) and broke the arrow in half. Didn't even break the skin on his neck. (Don't try this one at home either.)

Is the mind really that powerful? My dad set out to test a model that would harness the power of the mind to increase his success in sales. He read everything that he could get his hands on about the mind. The more he read about hypnotism, the more he realized that there was an underlying principle: the ability to allow yourself to disengage from your personal belief system. The results can seem magical and unexplainable, but the ability to disengage just might be your most powerful tool. You've had it all this time, but just didn't know how to use it.

My dad began experimenting with "affirmations" and, to a large extent, they worked for him. Affirmations is a technique of positive self-reinforcement ("You are going to own this guy in the wrestling match today." "You are going to give a fantastic speech.") that when used consistently can help you disengage from negative belief patterns and substitute them with positive ones. Prayers work similarly (e.g. when you thank God and those around you and focus on acknowledging the positives and blessings in your life.).

The Perfect Week concept came to my dad while he was listening to a speaker at a seminar who said that a person never does anything without first picturing it in his mind. You don't open or close a door without the picture going through your mind. You don't tie your shoes, take a walk, take a bite of food without picturing the act in your mind. The picture may be fleeting and unconscious, but that quick flash through the neural pathways always occurs.

> ### THE PERFECT WEEK
>
> Start off by writing a newspaper headline about your perfect week: PETER JONES BREAKS ALL-TIME SALES RECORD!
>
> Write it on Sunday night prior to the week starting. Close your eyes, picture the headline, see a picture of yourself with your hands raised like a prizefighter, and if there is nobody around to think you are a nut job, yell aloud, "YES! YES! YES!"
>
> If you don't feel shivers going down your spine, do it again and yell louder.
>
> A limiting belief system (you might not even know you have it) will make a successful sales career impossible. Beliefs are how you view the world. They are like eyeglasses filtering what you see. You can believe whatever you want to, but those beliefs are often influenced by external forces like your parents, your friends, the media, and of course your life experiences.
>
> You have the ability to create a new belief system, whatever that may be.
>
> You can do it right now as you read this sentence.
>
> You can believe that you can submerge your arm into a boiling pot of water and experience no pain, put the sharp tip of an arrow into the soft part of your throat and break that arrow by lunging against a wall, talk to strangers without fear and with complete confidence, and be the best salesperson there ever was.
>
> You can believe that your belief system is created by you, and that you have the power to believe the life and experiences you want into existence.

## DICTATING YOUR FUTURE SUCCESS—THE NOTE

This technique is also done on a weekly basis. Preferably on a Sunday prior to bed. At the top of a single piece of paper write the date of the following Friday. Imagine you are writing a quick email or note to your best friend, mother, wife, or anyone who really cares about you and your success. Start the note/email the same every week: "This has been a perfect week…"

When writing the note, keep in mind these three concepts:

1. Remember that "perfect" doesn't mean "ideal." Perfect actually allows your mind to make all things work together for good even though they may not appear at first glance to be good. Perfect is the long-term goal, and your mind will take an initial setback and turn it into something that works for you.

2. Use as many emotionally descriptive words as possible in the note about your vision. Describe in detail how certain meetings transpire or how you interact with your clients. Describe how your sales budgets get blown away. The more detail the better. Emotional words help the mind to not only see the result, but feel it.

3. Give this technique a chance to work. You may have some serious mental obstacles to overcome. For most people there will be some cognitive

dissonance (two separate self-images fighting for control of your future). People who have an easier time suspending their current personal status quo have always realized that there was something more to this life and they pursue that with acceptance and willingness. Others will take longer, but it will still work. Give yourself at least 12 consecutive weeks before you give up and go to work on a factory assembly line testing the quality of buttons.

Where do you want to be in five years, 10 years, 20 years? What you do today ripples into your future. If you do the same thing today you did yesterday, can you expect your life to be different in the future? Think you'll win the lottery? Think your ship will come in?

My dad won the lottery, or at least the monetary equivalent to the lottery, but he didn't even buy a ticket. It was perfect. Not exactly the way he predicted it, but it was perfect.

> ### PERFECT
> This was told to me by the CEO of a company I worked for—a man who matched his pursuit of business excellence with a passion for spiritual self-development. He consequently spent considerable time on an ashram in India doing meditation and yoga, and had his own spiritual guru there.
>
> His guru was an amazing cook and it was his habit to cook for his students every evening. He made delicious curries and perfectly round *roti* (an

India bread that is dipped in curry).

The CEO told me of one day when he watched the guru prepare the roti dough very carefully, kneading it for some time before he was happy with the consistency. Then, taking small round balls of dough, he would fling them into the hot kiln where they would stick to the wall, small perfectly round pieces of baking bread.

The guru threw his dough one by one into the kiln. "Perfect!" he exclaimed each time, and indeed, the dough formed in literally perfectly round circles on the wall.

Somewhere along the way he misjudged a throw, and the dough splattered against the kiln roughly, creating a sort of elliptical misshaped piece of bread.

"Perfect!" the guru shouted in delight.

Secret #14: **THE PERFECT WEEK**

**Dad's Story**
**VISION QUEST**

I wrote about the challenges of starting a cable network from scratch without experience, without a budget to hire trained and experienced salespeople, and without the time to do the necessary research to find and qualify sales candidates—from zero to launch in seven months while making 90 percent of the sales presentations myself. Days started at 7:30 a.m. and concluded at 10 or 11 p.m., six days a week. Sunday was for catching up on everything that was falling through the cracks, and I rested on days that didn't end in Y.

About three months into this project I'd had it. I was exhausted, which is a term I deplore saying, but I was flat out tired. None of us involved in the project were thinking well or acting like our normal selves. A few squabbles were breaking out in the late night meetings. When was this going to be finished or when were we going to finally get our first ad sales commitment?

One evening I was walking into our scheduled after-hours meeting and the operations assistant, Cynthia, noticed that I looked down and mentioned it. I told her I was just tired and that I would be fine with a good night's sleep.

Cynthia asked me if there was anything she could help me with. I thanked her but said that she probably had enough on her plate to keep her busy through the weekend. She said that she would be happy to help with letters (handwritten, sent through regular mail) because she knew that I did not have an assistant. I thought for a minute and asked her how she thought that Mark, her boss in operations, would like it if he knew she was helping write the hundreds of letters that we were sending out every month.

"Mark won't care, but I'll ask him just in case," she said.

"Don't tell him that I asked for the help."

She promised to tell him that she had volunteered.

About two weeks later Mark, Cynthia's boss and our head of operations, came to see me. Uh oh. Cynthia had been doing my projects almost daily. Phone calls, follow-up letters, and meeting planning. So when Mark showed up that early morning, I thought I had lost my helper for good.

Mark asked me how it was working out with Cynthia.

"Really good," I said cautiously, "but I don't think you are here to check on her performance?"

"Actually I am," he replied, "because Cynthia wants to get into sales and she asked me to put in a good word for her."

"Mark, Ken (our boss) is going to flip out." We had a rule that we were not ever to poach another department's personnel. Besides, I was hiring my own assistant in a couple of days. "I won't need her to help after I finish with my hire."

"No," he said, "she wants to get into sales; she doesn't want to be an assistant."

We talked for a long time and he was serious about helping her get a shot at sales, but she was young. She had no sales experience, and she worked for Mark. From my perspective, it was a nonstarter.

Ken called me a couple of days later to flip out.

"What are you doing going after Cynthia when you know better!" he screamed into the phone.

I told Ken that Mark had asked me to consider her. The fact that I hadn't gone after her did not matter to him.

"You can't," he said, "final answer."

The fact that I wasn't going to in the first place didn't seem to matter either.

Every day Cynthia would come by my office to share

Secret #14: **THE PERFECT WEEK**

with my assistant what she had been doing and ask her if she needed any help. I had explained to her our anti-poaching policy and that I couldn't hire her and she understood.

One day Cynthia picked up the phone when she was helping out, and it had been a prospect on the line.

I asked her to give me the number so I could call him back.

She said she already had spoken to him and that he was interested in advertising with us when we launched. She explained that he was going to be at the Hardware Show in Chicago and they wanted to meet her.

"Cynthia," I said, "do you know how much trouble you are going to get me in if I ask Mark if you can attend the Hardware Show?"

She said that she already asked him and he told her to go for it.

I couldn't let her go. Ken would have my head.

When I met the prospect at the show, he told me how helpful Cynthia had been. Wonderful. I was definitely going to lose my job over this.

Fast-forward. One of those early projects that Cynthia had worked on for me when I didn't have my own assistant was setting up an event in which we would present to over 250 vendors of the Lowe's Company. Lowe's was our first advertising commitment and they invited the vendors and we contacted all of them prior to the event to warm them up. Cynthia made many of those calls. We had 100 percent attendance. It was all hands on deck including many of the different departments, as we still only had about 25 employees. Ken was there along with all of the department heads.

At the event, Ken and I were talking with the president of Dutch Boy paints and Cynthia walked up to join us. Craig, the Dutch Boy president, looked at her name tag and almost shouted, "Cynthia, it is a pleasure to finally meet you in person."

What Cynthia said next completely stunned Ken and me. "Craig, can I count on your company buying at least two of these ad packages today?"

Ken looked at me and I shrugged.

"Are you my rep?" Craig asked Cynthia.

Ken said to Craig, "If you buy two packages she is."

Craig committed to two packages on the spot.

Cynthia helped me solve the biggest hurdle I had to hiring her when she closed that deal right in front of Ken. She went on to become my five-star salesperson. She had a vision for her own future and her commitment to her vision to become a salesperson made her fearless. She was highly successful because of it.

# Secret #15

## TRAIN THE BODY WITH THE MIND

*The most successful salespeople are relentless competitors who attack everything they do with the intention of doing it better than anyone else. Keeping a nimble, flexible, strong body will translate those same characteristics to your mind and significantly improve your ability to sell.*

When is the last time you went to the gym, sweated outdoors under the sun, or engaged in an activity so dangerous that you had to be 100 percent focused on it to avoid dying?

Work takes up an increasing amount of your day. Multinational corporations in the global economy never sleep, and they would prefer their employees not sleep either. Your smartphone demands your attention up until the time you fall asleep, and it's the first thing you look at in the morning when you wake up. And weren't you dreaming of work anyway?

You need a break. Not a vacation (although you probably could use one of those too), a break during your day that takes you entirely away from work. You need to work your body and give your mind a chance to rest and reflect.

Have you noticed how some of the most successful

people are also accomplished athletes, or just simply very fit? These are the busiest people you know, yet they somehow find an hour every day to swim or horse ride or practice hot yoga. This is partly because the most successful people are relentless competitors who attack everything they do with the intention of doing it better than anyone else. And it's partly because they intuitively know or have learned that the secret to a crystal clear and nimble mind is to work the body.

Do not think of exercise as something you have to do because it's good for you. That is a loser mentality that leads to short bursts of activity followed by long periods of sloth and self-loathing until the next short burst.

Think of exercise as one of the strategies you employ to practice winning. Think of it as one of the essential skills like listening to clients or overpreparing for meetings. Set yourself goals and celebrate when you achieve them. Surround yourself with mentors and support teams that will help you reach those goals.

Ideally, you should find a sports activity beyond the gym that is competitive in the sense that you will win or lose. To clarify what that means, first place is winner, second place is the first loser. The best salespeople love the elegance and simplicity of black or white, win or lose.

If you're reading this book, you compete to win, and if there's a chance of losing, you're going to train much harder than if not faced with the prospect of losing. What is closing a sale but winning?

## Secret #15: TRAIN THE BODY WITH THE MIND

> *Ideally, you should find a sports activity beyond the gym that is competitive in the sense that you will win or lose. To clarify what that means, first place is winner, second place is the first loser.*

Your days are crowded with conference calls at odd hours, client drinks and dinners after 6 p.m., business trips at hotels where the gym has mirrored walls, four dumbbells, and one of those big inflatable balls. When can you find the time to work out?

That's the wrong question. The question you need to answer is: When will you make time in your day to address one of the key areas that will make you successful? When you make that high-priority list every morning, exercise should always be on that list.

Let's address this in another way. Look at your entire day, and let's say you wake up at 6 a.m. and go to bed at 11 p.m. During that day, when is the time that you are most likely to be free from work commitments? Most of you will have three options:

1. First thing in the morning before work
2. Lunchtime
3. After work

You can pick whichever suits you best. Lunchtime is especially nice as it allows you to refresh and re-energize after your morning of work. That said, a lunch workout schedule is also the most difficult to be consistent with, as your schedule will be threatened by long running meetings, urgent issues that need to be addressed, or your boss asking you to get a bite with him.

After work is nice. You've worked hard all day, and work is still in your head on the ride home. Again though, it's easy to get derailed from that schedule by overtime, work calls with different time zones, exhaustion, and the craving for a slice of pizza and four pints of lager as soon as you leave the office.

Morning. Now morning is pretty hard for anyone to mess with. Lots of people get up at 8 a.m. for a quick shower so they can be in the office right at 9 a.m. Nobody knows when you wake up, and there is something a bit sacred about not calling anyone before 9 a.m.

It's practically the only time left in any day that you truly have full control over. And you can adjust just how much time you have control over simply by adjusting what time you wake up. If something is of utmost importance to you, we suggest scheduling it for first thing in the morning. Not just exercise. Has it been your lifelong goal to learn Spanish or play the piano? What if you had been practicing either for an hour every morning from 6-7 a.m. for the last ten years?

Many think they aren't morning people. Well, you can change that by instituting a task that you do every morning without fail. You'll get used to it pretty quickly. And it doesn't have to be morning if you absolutely can't do mornings. You could apply the same methodology to night—every evening from 10-11 p.m. is your workout time.

Imagine you are a wolf (put on the wolf T-shirt that you bought at the same time you bought that dream catcher).

## Secret #15: TRAIN THE BODY WITH THE MIND

The wolf is walking around the forest or wherever it is that wolves roam, and suddenly a bear comes charging out of the woods to attack the wolf.

The wolf doesn't do a few jumping jacks, pushups, and light stretches before engaging the bear. The wolf goes from walking around the forest zero percent to fighting the bear 100 percent in the blink of the eye.

This is what you are aiming for. Train yourself to wake up and be in the gym doing kickboxing five minutes later, to wake up and be conjugating Spanish verbs before you have had your first cup of coffee.

Imagine how this amazing ability to instantaneously go from zero to 100 percent can work for you in the business world. You are having a drink with your girlfriend at a dive bar and in walks Ross who you've been trying to meet for three months. Are you ready to say something compelling that is going to get you that meeting? Do you always have an elevator pitch for Ross that is Shakespearian in its eloquence on the tip of your tongue?

Keeping a nimble, flexible, strong body will translate those same characteristics to your mind.

### Son's Story
# THE LUNCH WORKOUT

It takes some serious swagger to walk out of the office at 11:45 a.m. holding a gym bag and return (slightly sweaty) at 1:30 p.m. But this is what I did for many years.

I practice Brazilian jiujitsu. This is something like wrestling, except that the goal is to lock your opponent's joints so that he has to submit (tap out) so that they don't break, or to choke him unconscious (ideally he taps before he actually goes all the way out).

This is not something, like the stair stepper, that you can do while reading a magazine. Someone sets a timer for five minutes and, when it starts, you engage in full combat with another person of roughly your size (sometimes smaller, often bigger) who is trying to cause you serious bodily harm. Tapping is losing, akin to a dog rolling on its back to show its belly. If you like to win, tapping is not something that is pleasant to do.

It was tough to get out of the office at noon to train, but I learned through trial and error that it was the most effective time for me. I am an early riser and would frequently start my day with 6 a.m. calls with New York and arrive in the office very early. By noon I had several hours of work behind me. And—because I prioritize my tasks to address the most important and challenging ones first—I always had dense and fulfilling morning sessions.

Training at lunch took me out of that and gave my mind a chance to refresh while my body stepped in. Regardless of how I felt when I walked into the gym, it was absolutely impossible to think about an email I needed to write while someone had their arm around my neck trying to choke me unconscious.

## Secret #15: **TRAIN THE BODY WITH THE MIND**

It was easy to get distracted and miss that lunch session, so I treated it just as I would an important client meeting. I scheduled out a 90-minute block of time from noon that I couldn't miss.

It helps to have a like-minded boss who will support that kind of schedule, but if you don't, simply come in a bit earlier and stay a bit later, and openly tell your boss that you would like to take a longer lunch because it makes you more productive in the afternoon.

Who were the other attendees at that afternoon training session? Senior executives at Goldman Sachs, bond traders at major firms, and other top executives who believed in cultivating a strong body to complement their strong minds.

# The Final Secret

Ben is based in Tokyo where he heads the Information Security team in Asia for a multinational financial services firm.

I hadn't seen Ben in years and we had a lot to catch up on. He told me about some of the projects he was working on, and mentioned a new system his firm had put in place that let him solicit requests for price proposals from several companies at one time, so that "I don't have to deal with shady salespeople."

"So you get online quotes from different providers and make your choice based on that?" I asked him.

"Right," he told me. "I never have to talk to anyone. All the information they need to quote me is right there."

"There's no customization when you roll out at different offices throughout Asia?" I asked him.

"Of course there are tweaks that we have to make here and there. That sits with the local teams though. It usually goes fine."

*Usually*? I still didn't quite get it.

"Let me make sure I understand. You and others at your firm dislike speaking to salespeople so much that you have created a system for which the entire purpose is to

# The Final Secret

execute a project without ever talking to a salesperson?"

"Pretty much, yes," he told me.

What dysfunctional thing happened in the past? What abhorrent behavior did the sales professional demonstrate that got us to this point? "This point" being the point where clients are actually making significant investments in systems for which the sole purpose is to avoid salespeople.

Ben went on to tell me that "most salespeople would be best handled by large caliber weapons." Perhaps he had forgotten that I am a career salesperson, and would rather not be shot with the gun that one uses in Africa to take down wild elephants. I decided that I probably wouldn't see Ben again for a while.

If your experiences being sold to have been so bad that you fantasize about violence towards salespeople, something about the buyer/seller relationship has gone very, very wrong.

Buyers take note: If your salesperson makes you feel like something is being done *to* you, you may want find a new salesperson.

Most sales methodologies are based on the premise that the salesperson is doing something *to* the buyer. Someone is selling, and someone is being sold. We can call this the "Do To/Done To" approach to selling.

I invite you to consider this key belief that can revolutionize how you think about sales: The client and the sales professional want the same thing. *A solution that feels like the natural consequence of a satisfying conversation.*

Are you with me on this? Can we agree that, at the

heart of the matter, both the client and the salesperson want the same thing?

The client wants a solution for three possible reasons:

**PAIN**—This is killing me and I want to move away from this pain.

**GAIN**—There is a huge potential upside and I want to move toward that gain.

**NOVELTY**—I don't know if this going to help me, but it's something new that I haven't seen before so I'm willing to explore further to find out.*

If you cannot identify a pain, gain, or novelty with your client, you are better off focusing your attention elsewhere. If you do not have pain, gain, or novelty, you do not have a buyer. If you do not have a buyer, you never have a sale.

> The client and the sales professional want the same thing. A solution that feels like the natural consequence of a satisfying conversation.

So that gives us some clarity as to why the client wants a solution. How about the salesperson?

The salesperson wants a solution for several different reasons perhaps. Some want to help their clients be successful. Some have quotas to hit, bills to pay, Hawaii vacations to take. Simply enough, most people want to do well at their jobs and salespeople are no exception.

---

*See *Let's Get Real or Let's Not Play* by Mahlan Khalsa and Randy Illig for a comprehensive and excellent description of this concept.

## The Final Secret

I would suggest one big reason trumps all this though.

At some point in the future, you—the sales professional—would like to sell to the same client again.

If your solution does not work in the way that you promoted it, the client will not buy from you again.

If your solution costs significantly more than you advertised it, the client will not buy from you again.

If you are arrogant and manipulative, or "hard sell" your client, the client will not buy from you again.

> *At some point in the future, you—the sales professional—would like to sell to the same client again.*

What we have proposed in this book is an alternative to Do To/Done To selling. We have instead offered a type of authentic selling that really bears no resemblance to the traditional sales engagement. In fact, this doesn't feel like being "sold to" at all.

This is Dad's final secret, and the holy grail of sales sophistication.

Sales doesn't have to feel like sales, and the highest and most sophisticated form of sales is so subtle, so rewarding for both parties that the actual "selling" is invisible.

That's right, invisible sales.

A type of selling where the sales professional listens much more than he talks, penetrating the invisible need of every human being to feel "heard" and be "understood."

A type of selling where the sales professional asks questions not for himself but for the client, to elicit new realizations and to envision a positive future.

A type of selling where the sales professional has mastered the subtleties of non-verbal communication and, therefore, reads and reacts to body language like having an invisible conversation.

And ultimately, a type of selling that results in a solution that feels like the natural consequence of a mutually satisfying conversation.

When a buyer is being invisibly sold to he doesn't refer to his sales guy as "my sales guy." This is not the world of vendor, seller, buyer. In this world the client calls his salesperson "my mate," or "my business partner," or "my trusted advisor."

> Sales doesn't have to feel like sales, and the highest and most sophisticated form of sales is so subtle, so rewarding for both parties that the actual "selling" is invisible.

As with anything, practice makes perfect. For example, you don't suddenly become a great listener who effectively employs silence in meetings. Listening is a choiceful act, so you'll need to make a choice each time you decide to listen. If someone tells you that he is always a great listener, he is delusional about what it means to be a great listener. Like building up a big bench press in the gym, it takes a lot of reps to get good at it. A hundred reps for the technique to become familiar. A thousand reps to really know it. Ten thousand reps to truly master it.

The same applies to becoming a great questioner, to role-playing, to becoming a religious chronicler of all your meaningful client interactions in a CRM system.

Understand the technique cognitively in your head first. Then practice it with your body to make it your own.

If you are trying to hit a quota, struggling with that Monday morning commit meeting ("How much are you going to sell this week?"), nursing a pipeline that is leaking water like a wood boat with holes, I feel for you. I've been there. My dad has been there. I'll be there again. That's what makes sales such a rush. You can never perfect the process. There will always be room to be better, to refine this or that, or to try something new.

At the very core of it all, what are you—the salesperson—really doing? "Sales" is not just about making a sale. It is about pinpointing your client's need and, as a trusted advisor, finding a solution to meet it.

Isn't sales all about helping your client succeed?

# In Closing

I had a period when I wasn't selling. My sales muse was cheating on me with my best friend. Self-doubt crept in. Like athletes, we sales professionals are only as good as our last big game.

I'd written about two-thirds of this book by then, and then set it aside for a year. When I was in that bad period I picked it up again and found glaring holes in my current sales practice. I hadn't been following my own rules!

Invigorated (and embarrassed, and a little pissed, well, actually more than a little pissed), I reread my own book closely, changed what I was doing literally overnight, and immediately went off on the extended sales run of a sales beast who has no natural predator. I sold inside of things that I sold and then I upsold two more.

No matter what your current level of sales mastery, I hope you will take at least one significant thing from this book that will help you sell better. It's a tough life, but damn, doesn't it feel good to close a deal?

Brian Newman
February 2015
Hong Kong

**BRIAN NEWMAN** is a certified Executive Coach (ICF) based in Hong Kong. Prior to founding his executive coaching practice, Brian was head of Asia ex-Japan Sales for Asia's largest executive coaching firm. Before that, he led the Asia sales teams at a Moody's Corporation subsidiary and at investment banking platform provider, Dealogic. Based in Asia for more than 20 years, Brian is fluent in Japanese and is a lifelong practitioner of the martial arts.

**STEPHEN NEWMAN** has a 30-year career in media and advertising sales, and in 1994 was part of the founding team that launched the American cable television channel, Home and Garden Television (HGTV). As global head of sales, he grew revenue from zero to $180 million over six years at HGTV, making it one of the most profitable independent television channels in the nation.

www.ingramcontent.com/pod-product-compliance
Lightning Source LLC
Chambersburg PA
CBHW071758200526
45167CB00017B/441